IRISH COUNTRY LIFE

Olive Sharkey is from the Irish midlands, near the site of the thatched farmhouse in County Westmeath that she recalls in this book. Her interests include photography, travel, nature and folk-life bygones – in particular, curiosities from days of old. She and her husband, Denis, formed their own publishing imprint, Magpie Publications, in 1989, which has published four books by Olive: *Nature Spy, Country Cameos, Four Swans Country* and *Fore and Its Ancient Buildings*. She is also a graphic designer and illustrator. This book was originally published in longer form as *Old Days, Old Ways and Ways of Old: Traditional Life in Ireland*.

Photos on previous pages: Women on road, Carraroe, Co. Galway, c. 1930; Donkey with panniers, Carraroe, Co. Galway; Children at Feohanagh, Co, Kerry, 1946

IRISH COUNTRY LIFE

OLIVE SHARKEY

THE O'BRIEN PRESS
DUBLIN

This revised edition first published 2020 by

The O'Brien Press Ltd,

12 Terenure Road East, Rathgar,

Dublin 6, D06 HD27 Ireland.

Tel: +353 1 4923333; Fax: +353 1 4922777

E-mail: books@obrien.ie. Website: www.obrien.ie.

The O'Brien Press is a member of Publishing Ireland.

First published in 1985 as *Old Days, Old Ways* by The O'Brien Press Ltd.

A revised edition, *Ways of Old*, first published 2000 by The O'Brien Press Ltd.

ISBN: 978-1-78849-184-6

Illustrations by Olive Sharkey

Photos courtesy of National Folklore Collection. © National Folklore Collection, UCD

Front cover photo: Harvest: Making a stack (oats), Dunquin, Co. Kerry, 1948

Back cover photos: Children at Feohanagh, Co, Kerry, 1946; Women in shawls, Carraroe, Co. Galway

Cover design: Emma Byrne

9 8 7 6 5 4 3 2 1

24 23 22 21 20

Printed and bound in Poland by Białostockie Zakłady Graficzne S.A.

The paper in this book is produced using pulp from managed forests.

Published in

DUBLIN

UNESCO

City of Literature

CONTENTS

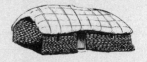

INTRODUCTION

When compiling this book I never intended to produce a study of Irish folk history or a detailed analysis of our recent past, but rather a compendium of old bygones. A lot of research was necessary, taking me into the musty and often cobwebby depths of folk museums where I became more and more intrigued with the range of bygones in the various exhibitions, and into the homes of fascinating elderly folk with surprisingly clear memories. My father, to whom I dedicate this book, was a mine of information and nostalgia about my own ancestral history, regaling me with yarns about life 'in the ould days'.

Many great writers and historians have expounded at length on the subject of Irish folk history in virtual tomes of information, but very few have contributed more than a few illustrations. It was this fact that first got me thinking about the possibility of compiling a book of old bygones – the tools, vessels and gadgets in everyday use when our parents and grandparents were children. Also, I belong to

Left top: The interior of a house, Maam Cross, Co. Galway, 1935;
bottom: Two boys on a boulder in a field, Glencullen, Co, Dublin

a family which was the last in our district to relinquish the old ways on the land and in the home. I have clear memories – happy memories – of seeing my father doing his farmwork with semi-primitive machines, of Dolly, the workhorse, and of seeing my mother churning the old way and fetching the water from the local pump in metal cans. It was a hard enough existence for them, but at least they had the comforts of a new, bright, airy home and electricity. My grandparents and their contemporaries didn't, at least not until they were too old to benefit from the improvements, so their lives must have seen a lot of hardship and drudgery. I wanted to document this as well to some degree.

Bygones tell their own story of how it must have been. I look at an old black kettle and am immediately transported back to a dark kitchen smelling of freshly baked bread and of turf smoke, with the solemn tick of a clock beating a slow tattoo in the background; and the sight of an old rusty plough reminds me of the smell of earth and the raucous whimpering of gulls rising and dipping behind my father as he slowly guided the horse and plough in other times. Other bygones, however, failed to inspire such thoughts simply because they were alien to me prior to researching this book, but perhaps they will evoke pleasant memories for others.

My research brought me to countryside museums in England and Scotland as well as Ireland. I found a lot of similarities between folk life in Britain and folk life in Ireland and, equally, a lot of interesting contrasts. Our social history made for different needs amongst the peasants, and our climate and terrain for a different type of vernacular architecture.

Our folk history is intrinsically ours and the bygones I've accumulated in this book are a very important part of that history and should not be ignored. I hope that by cataloguing them in this way I've helped to ensure their survival in our memories.

Below: Woman on Inis Meáin, 1925

FARMHOUSE FARE

When my grandmother was a young housewife she never complained of boredom, mainly because she was never idle. Each and every day was filled with bustling activity. In the home she had specific chores, but because she was a farmer's wife she was obliged to help out on the land whenever she could. Usually these extra chores didn't take up much of her time, but during the busy seasons on the land – haymaking and harvesting – she often had no spare time at all. When she wasn't out raking in the field or helping to wind hayropes, she was busily occupied in the kitchen with extra cooking and baking for the kindly neighbours who arrived daily to help get the crops saved. At these times of the year other mundane household chores had to be sacrificed for a while, but at no time could either cooking or baking be put aside.

In some homes, baking was a daily ritual, especially where there were large families, but in my grand-parents' home-baking was done twice or three times weekly. In many homes, oven bread was made, that is

Left: Bread-making using a pot oven in Co. Kerry, 1947
Right: copper jug

Left: griddle pan; below: sieve

yeast loaves, known as barm cakes, barm being the old term for yeast. My grandmother, however, didn't possess a wall-oven, so she made soda bread cakes in the pot-oven, and flat griddle bread. For variety she also made brown bread at regular intervals, currant cakes for Sundays and boiled porter cakes for special occasions.

The preparation of food was done three times daily. In the morning my grandfather and his family were treated to a hearty breakfast of porridge, known locally as stirabout, which was always made the night before, and a mug of tea each. Sometimes a second helping of porridge would be requested again at night in times of hard work on the land, when appetites were just as keen after dark as in daylight. The dinner was served in the middle of the day. It consisted of potatoes, or spuds, one or more vegetables from the garden and meat on most days. It was washed down with mugs of buttermilk, followed by tea and well-buttered bread. The 'tay', or evening meal, was served around six, though the time varied according to the work schedule – in summertime it might be as late as eight o'clock in the evening, in wintertime as early as four. It generally consisted of a fry – potato cakes with eggs and bacon in wintertime, something lighter in summertime.

July was a lean month in every farmhouse, including my grandparents'. Everything edible was scarce, including potatoes and vegetables.

Bread was consumed in large quantities, and porridge invariably took the place of potatoes in some of the poorer homes. In Lent too, when rural folk fasted voluntarily, hunger was known, especially amongst the children. My father remembered a time when the prospect of seeing yet more potatoes without the tasty addition of butter almost made him feel sick. And the bread was dry too, and remained so in many homes. Thankfully, my grandmother made jam whose tarty flavour took the misery out of eating at teatime at least.

As far as food was concerned, there was little variety at any time when my father was a boy. Rich desserts such as we eat nowadays were unknown, cakes were fairly basic – sometimes enlivened with alcohol by those who could afford such a luxury – and very little imagination went into the preparation of a main meal. Salads were unknown in most homes, whilst exotic foods from foreign parts were confined to condiments and spices, and of course the 'Ingan' (Indian) meal, a maize meal from India which had been introduced into Ireland during the Great Famine.

My father remembered having seen the maize meal in use when he was a small boy. It was yellowish in colour and came in three grades – fine, medium and coarse – usually in twenty-stone bags. The fine meal made passable porridge and the two coarser grades were blended into bread mixtures to create various alternatives to the soda bread and other traditional baked fare. For instance, Ingan ash cakes were popular in some homes. They were made by scalding a bowlful of the meal with boiling water fresh from the kettle, moulding it into a sloppy dough and adding salt liberally. Scone-sized lumps were removed from the dough and individually enveloped in cabbage leaves, then placed in a prepared 'bed' in the ashes. Half an hour later, the scorched leaves were drawn out with the poker, and when cooled sufficiently were opened out to reveal steaming, fragrant little cakes inside. They were transferred directly to the pan for a good slow frying in butter and egg yolk, and I'm told they tasted quite good.

In the home, the woman made the bread, but in the monasteries of old, the men moulded the dough and stoked the fires. Their methods were handed down, not to men but to women, who learned to use wall ovens and make yeast loaves with dextrous hands. Many homes in the midlands possessed wall ovens where yeast bread could be baked in batches once or twice a week. The dough was moulded in a wooden trough called a losset or losaid, some of which have survived and may be seen nowadays in museums, but in very few homes. It was left overnight to prove in the covered losset, expanding considerably and becoming pliable during that time. A long-handled oven-peel was used to transport the individual loaves to and from the depths of the brick-lined oven.

My grandmother's method of baking was simpler because it involved neither the proving of dough nor the handling of a peel, which could be tricky when the wall oven was very hot. She used a pot oven, a large, flat-bottomed, three-legged pot with a handle for suspending it above the flames in the hearth recess. The moulded dough, which incorporated bread soda instead of yeast as a raising agent, was placed in the pot, the lid drawn over it and then glowing coals heaped onto the lid when the pot was safely suspended from

the crane. The lid ensured that no smoke filtered through to the dough as it baked.

Soda cakes were generally crossed on top with a knife; my mother continued to do this even when such a chore was no longer essential. It was done in former times because the baked bread, which was crusty but white when it was removed from the pot oven, had to be toasted before the flames and traditionally housewives toasted it in quarters. Sometimes one quarter would be toasted at a time, as and when required. My grandmother had a harnen stand for toasting a complete cake of bread at a go, but she continued to cross her cakes anyway, a throwback perhaps to other days when her mother toasted the bread in the traditional quarters.

In medieval times bread was apparently leavened with milk, a tradition which is upheld even today in some rural homes.

Left: wooden toaster; below: long toasting-stick, designed to accept four farls together

But 'soured' potatoes – more than twelve hours boiled – were used too, as were the original true barm (a sort of yeast) made from oatmeal juice, as well as the traditional bread soda with a pinch of salt.

Oaten and wheaten flour and branmeal were widely used in all areas, but in parts of Wexford an inferior barley bread was made up to the 1800s. Oaten bread was widely used as a form of payment for goods or services in times of austerity. A cake known as harran bread – formerly *aran* cake – was known in the 1600s, and is said to have been made from a mixture of barleymeal and peas blended with an oatmeal dough.

Whitemeats, or dairy produce, have a long history in Ireland. Cheeses of various flavours, butter, curds and buttermilk, as well as fresh milk and cream, were consumed in vast quantities through-out history, and even today the Irish country folk are very fond of butter, milk and cheese. Hard cheese is relatively recent in Ireland, introduced when cheese-moulding became a part of cheesemaking. In fact, there are many stories of how people reacted when they saw hard cheese for the first time – most of them were certain it was tallow, for it looked and felt a little like it. Butter was made in every farmhouse, and when there was a surplus, wooden tubs of it were buried in the soft, antisep-tic earth of the bog. It was preserved there, slow to turn rancid, but sadly often forgotten about, for turf-cutters have frequently unearthed tubs of butter over the decades and were pleasantly surprised at how fresh the butter smelled, although few of them tasted it.

Butter was spread liberally on almost everything, even on porridge sometimes. Fresh herbs, onion tops and garlic were blended into freshly made butter to flavour it. Similarly, honey was used to flavour and sweeten porridge, which was served in a variety of ways by the more imaginative housewives. A milky porridge resembling gruel and flavoured with herbs was often eaten as part of the main course at midday when potatoes were scarce. Sometimes too, instead of serving porridge with milk in the normal way, the housewife served it with curds. And, when in season, wild fruits and nuts were added.

It is maintained that during the Middle Ages soldiers were sometimes paid with porridgemeal, and when they didn't have time to cook it they mixed the raw meal with butter – a mixture they called *meanadhach* – and took it on campaign with them to eat whenever they felt hungry. Garlic would have to be taken along too because the raw meal encourages worms in the body; garlic is an age-old remedy for dispelling them.

Sowans was a drink made from the husks of oats, a widely acclaimed thirst quencher when my father was a boy. It was made for the haymaking season when mouths were often bone dry if the weather was particularly warm. The husks were poured into a large earthenware pot, together with some whole oats, and left to soak in water for up to a week. The liquid was then strained through a rush mat ready for drinking. When buttermilk was used instead of water, the resulting liquid was boiled to form a jelly which was often used as an important ingredient in the traditional dish of flummery. *Práipín* was a breakfast dish made from griddle-roasted grains of wheat ground in the kitchen quern and served with cream and sugar. My father didn't know it, however, though he had heard of such a dish – by the time his parents were ready to get married, many of the old dishes were disappearing as the pan took over from the griddle.

It is generally accepted that the potato was introduced into Ireland in the 1590s; by the 1800s, many country people had grown to depend on it to a large extent, which is why the Great Famine was such a devastating experience in the middle of the nineteenth century. By the time my grandparents were setting up home at the turn of the century, the potato was still a very important part of the countryman's daily fare. It began to form the basis of many unusual dishes, such as potato cakes, or 'tattie' cakes as they were more usually called, and boxty, the traditional dish on All Saints' Day. For this latter dish, raw grated potatoes were blended with flour, milk and eggs and baked on the griddle. When eaten instead of bread for the evening meal, milk and salt might be added to the mixture, which was then known as dippity. Colcannon was one of my father's favourite potato dishes, served with onion tops normally, but with kale or

Above: baby feeder

Left: chestnut roaster

leeks at Hallowe'en, the traditional
boxty-eating time. Butter and
cream gave the mashed-up colcannon a
smoother texture, and in springtime, when nettle tops were blended
in for health-giving purposes, the dish was referred to as champ. Tat-
tie-oaten was made from a mixture of mashed potato, fine oatmeal
and melted butter and was a favourite with children. In wintertime,
another firm favourite was potato soup served piping hot, straight
from the skillet.

My father still used the old terms when talking about the potato.
For instance, a particularly small potato was a 'poreen' and was fed
to the hens, and a large floury potato whose jacket cracked open in
the boiling was known as a 'laughing spud'. He also recalled how
the potato dinner was always the favourite meal in his home years
ago, with everyone reaching hungrily for the spuds the moment my
grandmother placed them in their basket on the table. It was essential that everyone learned to peel their potatoes quickly or they might
miss out, the greedy, skilful peelers hoarding up little caches of spuds
on their plates before actually tucking in. Many a row started at the
dinner table, I was reliably informed.

Festive fare was a very important consideration when planning for
the various festivals during the year. One of the biggest celebrations
took place at Christmas, and for that no expense was spared. My

father related how Christmas was celebrated in his home when he was young. Preparations began well in advance of Christmas week itself. Food was bought in bulk, the house was given a thorough 'going-over' with dusters and brushes, and large-scale baking was done almost every day. However, nothing festive was consumed until Christmas Eve, when a specially baked fruit cake was eaten by the family shortly after the *coinneal mór* ('big candle', usually red) was lit and placed in the kitchen window.

Santy came during the night, of course; in those days, the toys in the sack were often home-made, and the traditional Christmas stocking was invariably filled with sticks of candy called 'Peggy's legs' and with lucky bags. Fruit, too, figured strongly, usually an orange or some other exotic fruit which might not be seen by the young-sters until the following Christmas. Early on Christmas morning, the frying pan would be heard sizzling over the flames in the hearth as the traditional Christmas morning steak was cooked for the man of the house. After early Mass, the housewife got to work on the preparation of the dinner. The goose or bronze turkey was cooked in the bastable pot (pot oven), bubbling away under a lid of constantly renewed hot coals throughout the morning. Outside in a nearby field, the men and *garsúns* (young boys) worked up an appetite with a game of 'shinny' (a rudimentary game of hurling) and went to their respec-tive homes in the early afternoon, feeling ravenous.

The man of the house was presented with the first huge mug of green goose soup, then the remainder of the gathering received theirs in tin panniers. The first course dispensed with, the family tucked into

the main dinner, which consisted of generous slices of goose, potatoes, vegetables and sometimes a thick, greasy gravy. Porter was served
to all age groups to wash the food down – a special concession to
the children in some homes on this important feast day. Afterwards,
porter cake was served with tea to anyone who could manage it.

The New Year was celebrated with a special barm brack, from
which the man of the house took three bites in the name of the
Blessed Trinity, then flung the remainder of the brack against the
cleanest wall whilst uttering a prayer for hunger to be banished from
the house for the coming year. The broken pieces were divided up
amongst the children and wife.

On the feast of St Brigid, 1 February, dairy produce was consumed in great quantities because St Brigid was the patron saint of
the dairy and therefore an important saint in farming communities.
Again a barm brack figured strongly, also applecakes, and colcannon
was made and eaten with noggins of milk.

Shrove Tuesday, the eve of the Lenten fast, was a day of self-indul-
gence where food was concerned – a veritable orgy of eating – as all
meats and meat produce were eaten in many and varied dishes. Since
the Lenten fast meant abstaining from eggs, milk and butter as well
as all meats and meat-based soups, the larders were fairly well cleared
out on Shrove Tuesday. The traditional way of using up the milk and
eggs was to make pancakes, the tossing of which above the flames
was a matter for competition amongst the young.

St Patrick's feast day (17 March) was an excuse for a break from
the forty-day fast. Meat was consumed in most midland homes on

that day, together with whiskey, ostensibly used for 'drowning the shamrock' amongst the menfolk. In parts of the west and south, fish was consumed instead, for many folk preferred not to break their Lenten fast at all.

On Good Friday, dry bread and water were eaten in deference to the Crucifixion, and no animals were allowed to shed blood. On Easter morning, when the fast was officially over, the children went out scouting for eggs, calling at each house in the district, begging for the eggs amassed during the previous forty days. They took them home, had them boiled and then took them to a selected little nook to eat them almost in secrecy. In the home, the father often consumed as many as six or seven boiled eggs on Easter Sunday morning, followed by a hearty meat-based dinner in the early afternoon and rich fruit cake in the evening. Corned beef was traditional Easter Sunday fare in some parts of the country, served with cabbage and spiced with saltpetre and juniper berries. For the young people who attended the crossroads dance there was a fruit cake known as prioncam cake (from *princeam*, 'capering') and, of course, porter and whiskey flowed liberally.

There were few festivities of any consequence during the summer months, but in the autumn the Harvest Home was a huge festival of eating and merrymaking in rural communities. It followed the harvesting of the cereal crops, a sort of thanksgiving festival to which friends, neighbours and all concerned with the harvesting were invited. Meat, barrels and half-barrels of porter, cakes galore and even *poitín* flowed in abundance.

On 29 September, the Michaelmas feast was celebrated with goose, and it also marked the killing of the so-called 'barrow pig' for winter use. The barrow pig was the largest in the group, and in my grandmother's time it was her job to monitor his progress up to the time of the killing, usually with a measuring tape. If he was below a certain size, he might consist of more fat than good bacon.

Hallowe'en was celebrated with the traditional barm brack, into which certain items were baked, in much the same way as they are today, with marriage divination in mind. Wild fruits, collected from the hedgerows (blackberries, hazelnuts, crab apples and damsons) also featured, but wild fruits collected after this time were not eaten because it was firmly believed that the púca (spiritual demon of the countryside) spoiled them after Hallowe'en night. The truth was that the early frost destroyed their flavour.

COOKWARE

Every museum I've visited has introduced me to many and varied kitchen gadgets and tools used in my grandparents' time. When describing them, the key word has to be utilitarian. Designs and materials were basic, but everything worked and was made to last. Some of the fireside paraphernalia used in baking and a variety of cooking vessels are shown on the following pages. The three-legged cast-iron pots were widely used in my grandmother's era, but are nowadays only seen painted black and serving as flowerpots. My grandmother had three of these – a large one in which the pigs' grub was boiled

Left: three-legged cauldron and skillet pot
Below: long-handled skillet (British in origin)

every night, a smaller one used exclusively for boiling the potatoes and a small one, called a skillet, which she used for boiling the porridge and sometimes for the cabbage or other vegetables. The skillet that is shown here was a long-handled English skillet, used a lot in the northern counties and around the Dublin area.

The griddle and griddle pan were used long before the frying pan found favour in the country kitchen. Griddle bread was a very popular alternative to soda bread. It didn't rise, so it had to be made fairly thick and spread evenly across the griddle space. I'm told it was quite delicious when freshly cooked, and easy to digest; freshly baked soda bread was notorious for causing heartburn in the elderly.

Kettles were generally heavy and black. As a child, I couldn't lift my grandmother's kettle even when it was empty, never mind when it was full. It was made from cast iron and was sooty black from the fire poking at its backside throughout the boiling. And it always seemed to be on, suspended from one of the pot-hooks on the crane and humming away quietly in welcome, no matter who arrived in. Copper kettles were popular too, especially as hob-kettles.

The roasting of the Sunday meat was a rare occurrence in most households because roasting equipment wasn't a feature of every home. For instance, the Dutch oven was known only in the better-class kitchens. The meat was hung from a spit device, then partially enclosed within a metal container, opening only to the flames. A spit-pan collected the juices as they slid from the revolving meat. The poorer man's alternative to this kind of elaborate spit was the horizontal open spit across the front of the hearth.

Containers were important for keeping food and ingredients dust- and damp-free. Salt, for instance, could become soggy if it wasn't contained in a wooden box close to the fire. A saltbox hanging from a nail on the wall was the norm; often it was a simple container fashioned from old pieces of wood, but sometimes a special turned container was used and placed strategically for maximum admiration.

On page 26 you can see a variety of other household containers. For instance, the cutlery-rack was often used instead of a drawer. Originally this would have been used in Wales, where love-spoons were collected and kept on display. Here, the container was modified to accommodate knives and forks as well. Flour was kept in large meal-bins, but small amounts of flour or porridgemeal were kept close to hand on the dresser lip in a container. When there was a parlour in the house, the polishing

Right top to bottom: hob-kettle; kettle trivet; Dutch oven and roasting-spit; spit pan

Left top to bottom: saltbox; pair of wooden noggins; cutlery-rack (Welsh in origin); plate-rack; Irish pewter measure

rags and polish and the black lead used for cleaning the old-fashioned range might have been kept in a kitchen 'tidy'. Racks were popular too – plate-racks suspended from a nail on the wall or standing beside the old-fashioned sink, egg-racks for keeping eggs tidy.

The dresser was occupied mainly by delph, but there were other things housed on its shelves too on occasion. Wooden noggins and piggins, for instance, which were used for holding milk and as porridge vessels. They were stave-built by the cooper and lasted a long time. Ingredient measures were lined up on a shelf too, and if farmers made their own herbal medicine or ground ingredients like ginger or nutmeg, usually bought whole, a pestle and mortar were essential.

Every kitchen had its share of gadgetry, a good selection of which is shown on page 28. My grandmother didn't have much time for such 'new fangled' ideas, restricting her gadgetry to a meat-mincer and probably a sugar-cutter, though my father could not remember having seen one in the house. Sugar-cutters were essential when sugar was bought in tall cones of solid crystal and had to be broken down with a hammer, then sliced. Coffee came in bean form, so a gadget was necessary there too – a coffee-grinding machine with a blade for grinding up the beans into a coarse powder. All kinds of squeezers were known – lemon and garlic presses, orange juice squashers, and meat presses which were used to make beef tea, a popular beverage with the older folk. Jelly was made from earliest times from bone stock and boiled calves' feet, most often for savoury dishes, but when honey was added it made a welcome sweet. Jelly made from aspic, which best suited moulds, was introduced in the 1800s, and jelly moulds fashioned from tin, copper and delph were used to create dramatic and unusual, if wobbly, shapes.

Small gadgets included cherry-stoners, marmalade-cutters, apple-corers, ice-shredders and bone-mills. And, of course, there was a variety of meat-mincers.

The knife-cleaner was perhaps the most unusual piece of kitchen equipment. In my youth, I had seen only the large table cleaner, whose internal wiry brushes cleaned the inserted knife blade when the handle was turned. But then in a local museum in Athlone I discovered a small, much more manageable knife-cleaner. The reason for having a knife-cleaner at all was because knives tended to turn black after continued use, and a cleaner which incorporated a grinding mechanism was an added bonus, for the knives tended to get blunt quickly too.

sausage-maker

meat mincer

early whisk and bowl

garlic press

all-purpose
kitchen knife

nutmeg-grater

lemon press

spice-grater with box

sugar-cutter

knife-grinder

pair of inhalers

coffee mill

meat press

nutcracker

knife

nutcracker

knife-cleaner

herbal-tea maker

Right top: meat-safe; middle: butter-cooler;
bottom: flour barrel

Keeping food fresh was a problem in hot, sultry weather. In the 'big house', an ice house might have been established somewhere in the grounds, but farmers who couldn't afford the luxury of a piece of ice, never mind an ice house, generally buried food temporarily in the coolness of the earth. Meat-safes, fashioned from wood with a wire-mesh panel in the door, kept meat and other perishables out of reach of flies in summertime, and butter-coolers and delph tureens kept butter and cheese reasonably fresh in the dairy.

Food was generally bought in bulk, especially flour, tea and sugar. My grandmother lived in an area where she could purchase a 'pennort' (penny's worth) of this and a measure of that – the size of the measure being predetermined by the shopkeeper. Tea might have been bought by the chest coming up to Christmas, and flour always came in flourbags, which were utilised afterwards to make flourbag sheets and vast aprons, while a good tea chest might become a clothes chest or end up holding tools in the barn.

The 'van' is still a feature of some rural areas, including my own. But in the old days it wasn't an engine-powered van, but rather an elderly hawker with a horse and cart. He touted for business in areas where farmers and others didn't get much opportunity to go shopping in a nearby town. His cart was always loaded with an unbelievable selection of stuff. For the housewife there were, of course, plenty of food items she might need, including pre-packed lumps of sugar, brown paper bags filled with tea, bread soda and other ingredients, as well as fly-ridden flitches of bacon, strings of sausages, enormous black puddings and other meaty items. Sewing needles, threads and other hardware would be included too, as well as panniers, tin cans and kitchen tools. My father and his young brother always made a beeline for the sticky penny-buns, eager to spend their hard-earned pennies on feeding themselves with the unusual confections.

On the once-a-month fair day, the children spent much of their time in the town, staring longingly at exotic foreign fruits, candies and confections in the shop windows. If they were lucky, they might get a length of tooth-shattering sugar-stick, or a Peggy's leg, or even some hard toffee. Both fruit and chocolate would have been beyond the reach of their pockets in those days.

Tea shops were great meeting places in local towns when my mother was a young girl, and, of course, the pub has always been popular with the menfolk.

Right: Thatched cottage, Carraroe, Co. Galway, c. 1930

HOMECRAFTS

Craftwork was an integral part of the rural community in early times because clothes and other cloth items were all home-made. Up to the 1930s, a travelling tailor made suits for men, and what the housewife could not make herself she had the local 'manty-maker' (from maintín meaning 'mantua-maker', a mantua being a cloak) sew up for a small fee. However, sewing was virtually obligatory for young girls who usually learned the craft at their mother's knee.

SPINNING AND WEAVING

Weaving is as old as civilisation itself, although the early looms were doubtless badly made and produced poor-quality cloth. Only the very wealthy would have had machines capable of pro-

ducing tapestries, fine rugs and soft fabrics. By the 1800s, ordinary farmers could afford the luxury of a good-quality loom, so that finer fabrics were being produced for the lower classes. The fibres used were

Left: Mary Barlow and her spinning wheel, Letterbrone, Co. Sligo, 1935
Right: at work on the spinning wheel

usually indigenous, such as flax (linen), wool and some wild cotton, although imported cotton was woven extensively around Prosperous, County Kildare, and imported silk was blended with wool to produce a fabric called poplin, woven in the Liberties area of Dublin and in parts of Cork.

Weaving was usually man's work. The raw material had to be spun into manageable fibres, and this was done by the womenfolk, who spun and carded. The spinner was often an elderly woman living alone and depending solely on the pittance her spinning brought in. If she was an efficient worker and was doing well, she could afford to buy her own wool from the farmer, but if she wasn't, she would 'steal' it from the hedgerows and fences where the sheep had lost hunks of their fleece in scratching or passing from field to field.

Sheep are resilient animals that thrive on poor land, and because of this the western half of the country has always been sheep-breeding country, and consequently spinning and weaving country. In the early twentieth century, the spinning and weaving industry was probably at its peak because, by then, almost every home in sheep-rearing country possessed a spinning wheel or a loom of good quality. The annual shearing, when the sheep were stripped of their warm fleeces, was an important event in the life of a farmer from the western mainland or from any of the islands along the western seaboard. The wool was collected, bundled into bales and sold to spinners, weavers or wool merchants, depending on the locality and the amount of wool. And, of course, some of it was kept for the farmer's own use.

The shearing took place from mid-June onwards, and different sheep produced different quality wools. For instance, Galway, Roscommon and Scottish Blackface sheep were all mountain sheep and produced long wool suitable for carpets and certain homespuns. Galway 'Muttons' and Wicklow Cheviots produced a medium wool suited to ordinary homespuns like shawls, petticoats and tweed for men's suits. But the Suffolk Down, a popular English introduction, was strictly a lowland breed with dense, short, thick wool, ideal for sorting and with very little waste. Fine tweeds were made with this type of wool.

Once the shearing was completed, the farmer graded the wool. A single fleece produced three distinct grades – the 'diamond' quality wool from the animal's back, the 'lesser diamond' from around the legs and above the tail, and the 'stragleens' from the very edges, which was invariably discarded.

The spinner washed the wool. The fleeces were carted to a nearby stream or well and washed as one might wash clothes, until all pieces of briar, mud, dung, dead leaves and grass were thoroughly removed. The fleeces were swished in the water to avoid tangling and felting, two serious problems which developed when wool was badly treated.

When the wool was dry, it had to be oiled. This could be done with goose-grease or, in more recent times, with paraffin oil, and was necessary if the fabric was to be waterproof. If coloured fabric was desired, the dyeing process took place before the oiling. The ancient Irish peoples loved bright colours and these they derived

Right: wool comb

from natural sources such as roots, leaves, berries and flowers, all of which produced a harmony of colours which no chemical dye of modern times can rival. Among the plants used were lichens in Donegal and Mayo, collected by children from rocks and boulders to produce various even dyes called crottle and scratloch, and heather, which produced a clear yellow dye. Yellow flag iris produced a dull black, while dull red was derived from the wild madder plant. A deep blue came from a plant named woad or *gláisín*, and a plant named rud produced a crimson dye. Rich black was achieved by soaking the wool for a time in a boghole, or by boiling it in bog water. Chips of oak added to the water gave an even glossier black, and a mixture of indigo and urine produced a blue-black. The flowers of the ragwort (*buachallán buí*) or those of the gorse (*aiteann*), were used to produce brown. Oddly enough, despite the 'forty shades of green' in the Irish landscape, green dyes were hard to produce and, until the advent of chemical dyes, all the greens were dull lacklustre shades. Consequently, green was considered unlucky, especially where clothes were concerned.

When the plain or dyed wool was ready, the spinner settled down at her wheel to spin it into a continuous fibre. Prior to the invention of the spinning wheel, the spinner spun by hand with a spindle. A spindle – sometimes fashioned from wood from a tree of the same name – consisted of no more than a length of stick with a weight at the end,

Left: reel-winder

Right: large wool spinning wheel or *túirne mór*

usually a piece of glass or a stone, which was called a whorl and served as a flywheel.

The *túirne mór* was the big spinning wheel, or wool spinner. It consisted of a large wheel on a simple platform with the spindle works positioned at one end, directly opposite the wheel. In some areas, the platform was low, so the spinner could sit while working; in others, it was raised and the spinner stood beside it. The smaller treadle-wheel was used a lot in Donegal and the north generally, where it was originally introduced to spin flax. Twisting and winding-on remained two separate operations until the introduction of the U-flier, and the treadle meant even more improvement because the spinner's hands were free to work the wool at all times. By re-spinning she could produce two-ply wool for heavy garments, and if she were spinning for the local weaver she invested in a niddy-noddy or click-reel to skein the wool; otherwise she rolled it into balls and sometimes kept them on a reel-pole beside her. When using either the niddy-noddy or click-reel she measured the wool into skeins, weighing set amounts. She had to keep a mental record of the wool fed onto the niddy-noddy, but a click-reel kept turning until a certain number clicked and she knew she had enough.

Next came the carding, which was done with a pair of carding boards or with the seedheads of wild teasel tied to a makeshift frame. The carding boards had rows of little curved teeth which opened and straightened the fibres by brushing them between the boards. The fibres were then fluffed up and made to lie in one direction only, and were finally rolled by hand or by the smooth parts of the boards into a tube-like shape called a rolag. It was now ready for the spinning wheel.

Flax was next to wool in importance, and although a few sporadic crops were grown in the extreme south, it was mainly confined to northern counties. The crop was harvested when the blue flowers were past their best, gaited or stacked in the fields, retted (allowed to rot) in a lint-hole, and finally gaited again until the flax farmer was ready to cart it to the linen mill.

The scutching mallet was used to make the fibres more pliable, though a special flax-breaker was much more effective. The fibres had to be combed, and for this a hatchel was used. When it was removed from the hatchel, any remaining bits of fibre were known as tow, and were made into either candlewicks or burden-ropes. The flax was stored in bundles known as stricks until the spinner needed them.

Left top to bottom: wooden niddy-noddy used for winding wool; carding horse; click-reel; carding-boards; flax spinning wheel

In boggy areas, the poorest spinners collected bog cotton for spinning. They also used it for stuffing pillows when goosedown was not readily available.

The loom was the implement of the weaver, varying in size from the small handloom to the huge floorloom. Few homes boasted both spinning wheel and loom, for the

weavers generally worked as a small village community and the spinners worked from outlying cottages. In Donegal, Mayo, Galway and the Aran Islands, weaving was an important industry in the 1700s and 1800s and is practised today in many areas. A weaving community was generally made up of the spinners, a dyester (traditionally male) who dyed the wool expertly, and a group of 'clothiers' or weavers who lived close to each other or to a tuck mill, a small milling business powered by water.

Traditional Irish clothing, which survived up to the 1920s in some rural areas, was made from wool or linen, with ceremonial garments and some 'Sunday best' fashioned from silks or satins. Donegal produced practical tweeds, dyed dark, and often

Right top to bottom: flax beating machine; flax hatchel; small handloom; cottage floorloom and flying shuttle bearing stripes, checks and plaid patterns. Similar quality was produced in Mayo, but the colours were traditionally brighter. Galway produced the famous *báinín*, or white flannel, and of course Kerry homespuns were poorly regarded for they lacked imaginative design and decent colours, although Kenmare tweed was held to be very good.

NEEDLEWORK

Needlework incorporated the use of needles and included many different and specialised crafts. Sewing was perhaps the most basic needlecraft, and in my grandmother's day virtually every girl could make her own clothes, although the services of the local dressmaker were called upon if a woman needed a costume or coat made. Few women had the benefit of a sewing machine at their disposal, or the benefit of electric light. A workbox or basket housed the needlewoman's paraphernalia – cotton reels, scissors, pins and needles, and so on. And some women had a chatelaine which hung from a button by a small hook and contained a thimble, scissors in a small case and stitch-picker. A hemming-bird or wooden clamp held material to the table when it was being sewn, and a wooden darner was used when darning socks or woollen garments.

Left top: heron scissors; bottom: chatelaine

Right top to bottom: crochet needle and 'Afghan'
square; hemming-bird; spool-rack

Patchwork was an important craft in the old
days. The needlewoman used a combination of
patches of old discarded garments, backed with
flourbags for extra support, to produce quilts, cush-
ions or shawls. My own grandmother did this type
of work, but her favourite patchwork involved cro-
cheted 'Afghan' squares sewn together to make a
quilt.

American 'log-cabin' patchwork was known
in Ireland as folded work, and calico or flannelette was used as backing. Mosaic patchwork consisted
of geometrical shapes and looked like a neat jigsaw when finished.
When octagons or other awkward shapes were desired, they were
first traced on to cardboard and cut out so that the shapes would be
roughly the same size throughout the pattern.

Appliqué patchwork set no rules. Total freedom of design meant
that this type of work suited all standards of needlework, both the artistic and the clumsy. Motifs such as
birds or flowers cut from chintz were common, and
the edges were always left 'raw' with herringbone
stitch finish.

Quilting – not to be confused with patchwork quilt-making – was another old craft. The

quilt was made by securing three layers of material together by through-sewing stitching in decorative patterns. A pricking tool marked the patterns beforehand.

Whitework flourished throughout the 1800s. Muslin was a favourite material for summer garments at that time and lent itself very well to embroidery of this kind, incorporating white sprigs or even more elaborate patterns, always in white.

Men's suits were invariably made by the travelling tailor. Some clothing could be purchased at the stalls on fair day, but these didn't always fit correctly, so, when possible, suits were made by the tailor. He arrived in the district from time to time, bringing with him his goose-iron, his special ironing-board if he had one, and his box of needles and other tools, and it was traditional for the client to provide board and lodgings as part of the fee for the suit.

LACEWORK

Whitework, already described above, was a form of needlepoint lacework, but genuine lace was made on a cushion with bobbins and was called pillow-lace in Britain and bone-lace in Ireland, probably because the earliest bobbins were made from bone. The pillow was well stuffed with feathers or hay; tightly packed straw was the favourite material. The centre of the pillow sagged with use and often had to be 'middled' (refilled at the middle). When not in use, it was covered with a protective dust cover called a heller or hindcloth.

The pattern for the lacework was pricked onto parchment with an old needle fitted into a wooden bobbin, and the pins which followed the pattern were always rust-resistant brass and were known by various names, such as limmicks, bugles and kingpins. The bobbins varied considerably, but all were decorative, often enhanced with coloured beads, shells, etc. Domino bobbins were decorated with little spots. A young man often had 'I love you' or some such message inscribed on a bobbin for his lady-love.

A bobbin-winder was used to feed thread onto the bobbins, but this was a luxury most lacemakers didn't have. Instead they wound the thread by hand, a long and tedious job.

Embroidered net, such as whitework, was known as Limerick lace, and in the area around Carrickmacross in County Monaghan, lacework known as cutwork was made by sewing through a sandwich of paper pattern, muslin ground and machine net. When the sewing was completed, the pattern was torn away and

Right: lacemaker's pillow

the muslin cut to leave a delicate sprinkling of flowers or whatever on the net. In the area around Mountmellick, County Laois, yet another type of whitework was known: a strong, white, cotton thread was worked on a linen base to sketch delicate floral patterns.

RUSHWORK AND STRAW SCULPTURE

In some parts of the country, particularly damp localities, rushes were used in craftwork. Principally they were used for making St Brigid's crosses to celebrate the feast of the patron saint of the dairy on 1 February, and although similar rules and traditions were known throughout the country, different crosses were known in different regions. The rushes had to be pulled and not cut – that was essential if the charms it was to carry were to work – and it was important that they be pulled on the eve of the feast day. The girls made the crosses, then sprinkled them with holy water and placed them above the door, on the dresser and in the cow byre. Traditionally, three-legged crosses were hung in sheds in the northwest, and when rushes were not available, straw or some other material sufficed.

Straw was used in the fashioning of corn dollies for the harvest celebrations in autumn, when boys were encouraged to present them to girls. Nowadays they are still made in Britain for sale in craft shops and I managed to pick up a traditional lantern dollie, which was known

Left: corn dolly

here too. Oaten straw was simple to use but too soft to last long, and barley straw was too short to work with; both wheaten straw and rye straw were long and excellent for plaiting.

TRADITIONAL IRISH COSTUME

Traditional Irish costume, or peasant costume, was determined by the hardship endured. Shabby clothing was the norm on land, even for the womenfolk, and the children were often forced to dress in cut-down adult clothing or cousins' cast-offs. I can remember seeing my grandfather clad in hard-wearing striped shirts, heavy-duty but shabby trousers, tied at the legs, and hobnailed boots. And my granny wore a black shawl, heavy-duty flared skirts, big starched apron, a couple of wool jerseys and black boots or laced shoes. Paisley frocks were popular in the summer when the weather was hot.

The hooded, Kinsale-type cloak – black with red satin lining in the hood – was popular during the nineteenth century. *Báinín* cloaks were common in the west, while on the Aran Islands a beautiful shawl was worn. Red or blue striped petti-coats were worn with the 'linsey-woolsy' or drugget skirt, both of which came to within five inches above the ankle and no higher until the early 1900s. Black druggets often doubled as shawls.

Right: Aran woman wearing drugget skirt, which doubled as a shawl in emergency

The white lacy cap worn by married women was known as the *caipín lása* ('lace cap'), and a *binneog*, or kerchief, was worn when out working in the fields. In summertime, sun hats woven from rushes and muslin bonnets were popular, especially with young girls.

Among the curiosities were the 'Paddy Martins' or footless stockings, which my grandmother knew as *troighín* (from *troigh*, meaning 'foot'). They were designed for wearing in wet weather when continuous flapping of a wet skirt against the legs could cause blistering. In boggy areas, pattens or leather brogues mounted on platforms were worn when traipsing over peaty land. Leather shinguards called leggings were used when working in the fields. They were drawn over flapping trousers to prevent them from getting in the way of dangerous machinery.

The Aran Islands had their own distinctive costume. The men wore sailor-type trousers with a slit on the outer side of each leg, thus enabling the men to pull them up over the knees when wading in the

sea. Flannelette shirts and chunky, oily Aran sweaters were worn to keep the strong winds and rains at bay. Each family was known to have its own combination of Aran stitches so that a fisherman washed ashore following an accident at sea could be identified. The *crios* was the traditional woven belt

Left top: patten, used to raise feet above soft mud or bogland; bottom: pampootie shoe (Aran Islands)

for holding the trousers secure, and pampooties were the leather slippers worn on the feet.

Mainland people once wore rawhide slippers similar to the pampootie. They were made by the brogue-maker from a single piece of rawhide called a kip, and sold in large quantities at the local fair. Clogs with wooden soles were also worn in some areas, and some clog-making tools can be seen in Knock Folk Museum, County Mayo, and in Muckross House Museum, County Kerry.

In more recent times, flourbags were made into shifts for young girls; cotton was fashioned into smocks like those worn by men in rural England up to the 1800s, and wool was knitted into all kinds of garments. In those days of self-sufficiency, nothing ever went to waste – even an old discarded jacket was taken to the field and mounted on a pole to scare the crows away from freshly sown seed, and old woollen garments made excellent floor cloths!

Repairing a thatched roof on Achill Island, Co. May, 1941

THE THATCHED HOUSE

The traditional Irish thatched house is perhaps one of the most appealing and most evocative sights the modern-day traveller in Ireland will meet. Yet, we must go deep into the hinterland before we encounter such a sight, and even then it will be less than authentic, for most thatched houses today play host to a whole gamut of anachronisms, such as furniture which rightfully belongs in what used to be called the 'big house', and electricity, which undoubtedly enhances the life of the modern house dweller, but doesn't – strictly speaking – belong.

The thatched house is virtually extinct as a 'natural' feature of the Irish countryside for two reasons: firstly, modern housebuyers want modern homes with modern amenities, and secondly, thatched houses are surprisingly expensive to maintain. For one thing, the cost of employing a thatcher to service the roof on a fairly regular basis is colossal. In the past, good thatchers were two-a-penny in the rural

Above left: pre-Famine peat cabin;
right: a chimneyless pre-famine stone cabin

areas, but nowadays one would have to travel a long way to find a skilled thatcher, especially one who is prepared to exercise his talents in all weathers.

The history of the thatched house as we know it doesn't go back as far as one might expect. Such houses began to be built probably at the end of the seventeenth century. It is generally believed that many of these early homes were erected within settlements now referred to as *clacháns*, a few of which survive today in isolated, underdeveloped parts of the country. Basically, a *clachán* was a small cluster of houses in a farming community, and the farmers worked the land surrounding the *clachán*.

During the eighteenth century the small farmers of Ireland were experiencing relative peace, but small outbreaks of famine and stress due to crop failure occurred with ominous regularity, culminating in the Great Famine of the 1840s. We are all well aware of the strife and misery the Famine brought in its wake and the serious setback it caused to what little development was being made in rural areas. It took the survivors a long time to get back on the road to improvement again.

By the early twentieth century, when my own grandparents were setting up home, virtually all farmhouses were rectangular in shape and were built with great attention to detail and even a small degree of flair, and finished off with a neat canopy of thatch which looked

Right: inland cottage (midlands)

particularly beautiful when it was first put on and still a lovely shade of burnished gold. Much pride was being taken in the general appearance of the home, both inside and out, and geraniums in big, black, three-legged pots held court outside many a front door and sprawling creepers clung to the front walls just as they did to the front walls of the 'big house'.

I have some fond memories of my grandparents' house, and of childhood days spent virtually under my poor granny's feet. My memories are twofold: of the happy days when the house was a home and my granny was in residence, and the sadder days when the house was being razed to the ground soon after she died. I can still see in my mind's eye the great thick external walls as my father brought them slowly to the ground, using just a pick, a shovel and a big iron bar. And I can remember the acrid smell of the rotten thatch.

BUILDING THE THATCHED HOUSE

When a new house was being constructed in those days, they didn't have to wait for planning permission or any other bureaucratic non-sense! They would simply choose a site and a few friends would vol-unteer their help for a couple of months, the time it took to erect the house. The whole exciting business would then be the main topic of

Left: wattle-and-daub chimney breast of ruined eighteenth-century cottage

Right: structural details of walls (midlands). (a = sods, b = wattle-and-daub, c = stone)

conversation and speculation for miles around.

To the casual observer the traditional Irish houses all look alike, but a closer examination will reveal not only superficial differences, such as different thatch finishes, but also structural differences, not apparent until the buildings are being knocked down, and differences in the layout of certain features within the buildings. Some houses, for instance, had bed alcoves incorporated, others had a dairy built onto one end, and so on.

Some early thatched houses were built on virtually no foundation at all, but most of those constructed since the early 1800s had strong stone foundations. The trenches were dug out by hand to a depth of up to two feet and filled in with stones and mortar or clay to bind them. The hearth wall was continued up to roof level in stone, and sometimes even the external walls were constructed from stone, or a mixture of stones and mortar. Clay figured strongly in the midlands, where it was easily acquired, and usually the internal partition walls were built from a mixture of wattles (interlaced rods and twigs) and muddy clay – a mixture known as wattle-and-daub. Clay was some-times used in the construction of the floor too, although flagstone floors were more popular, especially in farmhouses, because they were easier to clean. However, a besom or broom could remove the top

Right: coupled rafters on ruined house

stratum of clay from a clay floor in just one sweep.

Roof frames differed considerably from region to region, with less perceptible differences within districts. Bog oak was used in the construction of the rafters, being both strong and durable. The coupled roof was widely used and this is how E.E. Evans describes it, in relation to houses in the north of Ireland, in *Irish Folk Ways* (Routledge: London, 1957):

> The coupled rafters are joined by one or two cross-ties secured by wooden pins, and pegs driven into the rafters hold in place the long purlins which support a layer of branches or thin laths of bog-fir. On these rests a warm blanket of carefully fitted sods (scraws), an essential element of the traditional roof, keeping out cold and damp and serving as a hold for the rods (scollops) with which the thatch, over the greater part of the country, is secured.'

The practice of insulating with sods was followed also in the midlands, although not in other parts of the

Right: internal view of coupled rafters

country. Such insulation ensured that the house was warm and snug during the icy months of winter and remarkably cool in summer. I often heard my father say that the thatched house was the coolest place to be on a warm summer's day.

The features of the house, such as windows, doors and so on, were determined not only by personal preference on the part of the owner, but also by tradition and by necessity. Window openings, for instance, were always very small and few in number, a tradition born of necessity. Prior to 1800, window taxes were levied on the number and size of windows, and those who couldn't see their way to paying very much made sure they allowed only the minimum amount of daylight and fresh air into the home. Consequently they might develop typhus due to lack of fresh air, and deaths from this disease were not unknown. The tax became known as the 'typhus tax' as a result.

The traditional half-door was a common feature in some areas, yet was unknown in others. Its advantages were important, especially where the windows admitted little light or air. It allowed a good deal of

both daylight and fresh air to filter into the house, whilst at the same time keeping hungry hens out and crawling babies in. It also served as an armrest for the farmer while he smoked his 'baccy' and chatted to a passing neighbour. And when he was inside, seated by the fire, it afforded him a fine view of visitors as they approached the house.

Left: the half-door

Right: thatched mansion

All thatched houses, with the exception of some of the thatched mansions, were a single room in width, and anyone who added to their home by extending it in any other direction was doomed to a future filled with bad luck!

The thatched mansion was the forerunner of the Georgian farmhouse, and was invariably the property of the local 'big-shot' farmer in the district. There was just such a house in our townland, a fine rambling old house which was abandoned for a modern farmhouse as recently as twenty-five years ago or so. It was spacious inside, with a dozen fine rooms, including a rather primitive bathroom and a larder. The imposing façade suggested a mansion but, when examined from the side, the building showed itself to be a single room in width.

And at the other end of the scale there were the tiny one- or two-roomed houses. The poorest of these were the hovels constructed in the bogs by the turfcutters for their own use. Fashioned crudely from

Below: bogman's peat cabin and plan

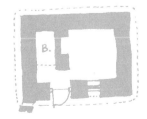

sods of turf and roofed with a covering of heathery thatch, they just about kept the winds at bay. On very cold nights a pole with a bundle of hay tied to it was drawn into the narrow doorway; rarely was there anything resembling a window, and if a chimney existed, it was only a hole in the roof.

A turfcutter invariably fashioned his own new home from bog scraws (sods), which often played host to families of pismires (a sort of bog ant). These busy little creatures had no qualms about sharing a hovel with its builder, which was fine so long as they kept a safe distance from each other! When they came in close contact, the pismire showed its displeasure by emitting a strong stinging acid, which didn't exactly endear it to the turf-cutter. However, the turfcutter was a quiet man and probably accepted the pismire as an occupational hazard.

Another type of thatched house, sometimes found in Donegal and often referred to as the Donegal longhouse, was a stone building built on a slope, with the slope built into the floor as well. The building housed man and beast together, and the slope was concentrated in the lower end of the two-roomed building – the part occupied by

Below: Donegal 'longhouse' and plan. (br = bedroom, k = kitchen)

the animals. The family lived in the same
room and slept in a second compartment
beyond the hearth. The cows and other animals spent the winter in the house, enjoying
the heat from the open hearth and a warm bed of straw, while the
humans chatted not ten feet from them.

Drainage in this kind of house was not a problem. Sunken floor
channels, sloping away from the centre of animal occupation, provided adequate drainage, while external channels took the waste
matter from the wall of the house to a pit a good distance away, usually alongside the dungheap in the yard. This custom of housing man
and beast together is believed to go right back to prehistoric times,
with the most recent example of this particular housing arrangement
visible on the island of Inishbofin.

THE THATCHER (*TUÍODÓIR*)

The rural thatcher was an important craftsman; his services were
required at all times of the year, not alone for roof thatching, but also
for rick thatching, which was important in the wealthier farming
communities. The craft of the thatcher was one which 'many men
could do, but few could do well', and it often took a thatcher many

years of trial and error to accomplish a skill of which he could be proud.

The thatcher was his own master, hardy, tough and independent, with no two operating in exactly the same way. Sometimes their work could be recognised individually, some displaying simple techniques and plain sensible work, others displaying ostentation and clever but painstakingly accomplished gimmickry. During heavy rains and other bad spells of weather when the thatcher couldn't work on the roof, he spent his time usefully making scollops (*scolbacha*). These were also known as rods or spars, and the slightly longer ones as sways. In some areas, scollop-making was an important local industry, the sole concern of one man who worked in liaison with all the local thatchers, and in those days there was one in nearly every townland. However, some thatchers liked to work independently, cultivating their own sally or hazel coppice. Essentially the scollop was a twisted length of sally (hazel in the midlands), pointed at each end and used to secure the thatch on the roof. Woodworm

Left top to bottom: thatcher's knife; trimming knife;
thatching spars or scollops
Right: spurtles, used for patching

sometimes attacked wooden scollops and to overcome this in recent times lengths of tempered steel were used instead. A wooden mallet was used to hammer the scollops home, and a sharp knife was all that was needed in their preparation – except for the twisting, which was done under the influence of steam.

There was a resident thatcher in almost every townland in the days of the thatched houses. There was one living practically next door to my grandfather, but being an independent sort of man my grandfather almost always did his own thatching, drawing from his slowly acquired knowledge of the skill. However, when the roof needed a completely new application, that merited the summoning of the local craftsman with his considerable knowledge and adroitness.

A good thatcher relied more on practical experience than on the acquisition of a few technical tricks. All aspects of the job, right down to the handling of the straw, required a quick and steady hand and a keen eye.

To the casual observer the thatched roof of the traditional Irish home is the same throughout the country. This is not the case, however, because different materials are used in different parts of the country and different methods of applying the thatch must also be taken into consideration. In my own locality, oaten straw was widely used in the old days, just as wheaten straw was used in wheat-growing areas. In the west and south, especially in the poorer regions, heather was often the only material to be had, and marram grass was used in coastal districts. Flax thatch was known in the north where the linen industry flourished, whilst rushes had to suffice in waterlogged areas.

Wheat for thatching was harvested when still slightly green so that the stalks would not be too brittle, thus yielding much more easily when handled. Some thatchers preferred to work with the straw from the winter crop and it was essential that the straw had been flail-threshed and not put through the threshing-machine, which would damage it considerably. The best straw, in fact, was that which had been threshed by hand against a rock or threshing-frame.

The coastal thatcher encountered different problems from those inland. The buildings on the coast demanded a greater degree of security and reinforcement in their roofs because the gales which swept in from the sea on a regular basis could cause havoc otherwise. Inland the problem was birds and their propensity for tearing at the thatch with their beaks and claws in an attempt to root out food in the form of grubs.

I can remember my father coating the thatch on my grandparents' house with a wash of bluestone to keep the birds at bay; apparently

Below: coastal farmhouse

they didn't care for bluestone, though a few bold crows disregarded it with haughty disdain and proceeded as planned. A scarecrow might be made as a last defiant gesture and erected above the front door, close to the chimney, in a fairly strategic spot. My father related a story of how his sister almost fell in a faint when she arrived home one evening at dusk to find 'an ould man' climbing up the roof, apparently with sinister intent. My grandfather had erected it that day and was greatly amused by her reaction!

Methods of thatching were determined not only by climatic conditions, but also by the material used and by the skill of the craftsman. A good thatcher took great pride in his work, and when passing houses he had roofed, little else would occupy his thoughts. A householder who didn't show active concern when his roof seemed to be rotting away would incur the local thatcher's wrath and an argument would ensue should the two ever meet. It was usual for the thatcher to return to his clients once in every five or six years to patch the roof, and every ten to fifteen years to renew the entire canopy.

In coastal areas, where the thatch had to be secured with ropes and weights, the thatched roof often looked very attractive with its crisscross pattern of ropes, or in more recent times of tarred string. This lattice-work was popular in parts of Donegal, Mayo and Galway, but in other parts of Donegal and in the far north generally, the ropes were invariably fixed vertically to the roof. Originally woven from sallies, hay, straw or, for greater security, bog deal, these ropes were superseded by sisal in recent times. The ropes were weighted down at the eaves by small boulders tied to the rope-ends on the gable walls only. Sometimes some of the gable stones projected beyond the wall surface to accommodate the rope-ends. Wooden pegs were used too, as were iron bars in more recent times.

The thatcher, like all other craftsmen, had his own specialised tools, some of which are shown on the opposite page. For instance, the yoke was used either to carry a burden of straw or to hold the straw in position beside the thatcher on the roof while he worked. The leggat was used to hammer the straw-ends neatly into position at the end of a stroke so as to give a clean finish. A long-handled shears or slash-hook trimmed the thatch at the eaves, but a shearing-hook was used for most other trimming jobs and sometimes even in the preparation of scollops.

Old Jack, our local thatcher, didn't carry many tools. From what my father could remember, he relied almost exclusively on one knife, a small mallet, a handmade rake fashioned from a length of wood with nails hammered into it and a thatching needle. The needle was an essential tool which the thatcher used to stitch the thatch to the roof. In parts of the west where tarred string was used instead of straw, the string was stitched in and out through the rafters as well as the thatch, which meant that an assistant was required, working from inside by crouching in the loft. His job was to keep an eye on the ties and return the needle through the thatch. Usually for this job a special needle was required.

Left: plastered gable with stone rope pegs

When my grandfather was expecting Old Jack to do a job for him he generally prepared the straw himself. This had to be done some time in advance. It was carted from the stack in the haggard, unloaded and shaken out in the yard and subjected to a considerable drenching with water. A timber plank was placed on top of the sodden mess, left overnight, then removed in the morning as soon as Jack arrived. Jack's first job was to climb the ladder to the roof and remove all the decayed thatch which was to be replaced. My grandfather would then assist him when the actual thatching got underway. Grandfather was the puller, which meant that he stayed on the ground and pulled bundles of straw from the pile in the yard. He pitched the straw up to Jack who placed it alongside him on the roof, preparatory to working with it in manageable amounts known as yolms. These were barely handfuls, and the first few were often referred to as 'bottles' and were placed in doubled layers along the roof at the base, their butts hanging out over the wall. Single layers were subsequently applied to ridge level. Jack, like most other thatchers, commenced thatching at the bottom

Right top to bottom: thatching needles;
leggat, used for tidying straw ends;
thatcher's yoke; long-handled rake;
shearing clips

right-hand corner and worked a width of approximately three feet at a time. Known as a stroke, this was said to be a comfortable width and was more or less standard.

Jack worked in all weathers, except perhaps during high wind, blizzard conditions and heavy rains, and it was a delight to watch him during the summertime. He usually worked for about a week at any one major surgery job, and wore what he called a spangle of straw around his legs just below the knees, presumably to protect himself from the spikiness of the straw.

Jack was a good thatcher, but not a very imaginative one, preferring just the one row of decorative scollops at the ridge. This was the practice with many Irish thatchers, whereas in England ornamentation was used to a greater degree. However, in some northern areas of Ireland and in the east, there seems to have been a happy medium, with some ornamentation and such embellishments as straw cocks and other creatures. Lattice-work was popular in the north, where it sometimes ran along below the ridge and again just above the overhang.

Thatch is the lightest of roofing materials and is highly inflammable. Yet in the old days it rarely caught fire. Steam engines posed the greatest threat when they visited with threshing mills, for they were generally parked for hours on end in the yard, spitting and hissing furiously and sending out the occasional spark which could readily lodge in the thatch. The roof would not catch fire immediately, but would smoulder quietly for days until a breeze suddenly set it ablaze and the whole building seemed to be a hot conflagration. A careful owner might have a fire-hook ready for such an eventuality, averting the fire by removing the smouldering thatch.

Gutters were unknown on thatched roofs; instead the rain was thrown from a generous overhang and drained away by sloping ground. In the case of poor overhangs, the rain invariably trickled down the exterior walls, creating a green stain in time, just one of the few disadvantages associated with living in a thatched house.

FURNITURE AND FITTINGS

Furniture in the average home in Ireland was always basic and functional, and often home-made. Most of the decorative pieces appeared at the end of the last century.

Kitchen furniture was crudely fashioned without great attention to detail, and if the house owner was not inclined to do such work, a 'handy' neighbour doubtless obliged and was invariably recompensed with a pair of chickens rather than money. A calf might be exchanged for something as big as a meal-ark or settle-bed, and a beefy bullock or the equivalent was a fair price for a well-made dresser or press-bed. An established carpenter, on the other hand, would have a set price and, unless he could accommodate animals or chickens on his plot of ground, would expect money.

The three-legged stool (*stól trí chos*) is no longer a feature of the country kitchen, but it is nevertheless familiar to most of us. It began its long history in the smoke-filled, chimneyless homes of ancient times, establishing itself there as a low 'creepie' (*stóilín*). It was essential for the family to squat low below the smoke level, so

Left: Dresser in farmhouse, Carbury, Co. Kildare, 1935
Right: Ulster hinged table and ladderback chair, with low, wooden, three-legged stool

the creepie was developed for the average man or woman. A particularly tall person would have been forced to squat at ground level on a rush mat to avoid getting watery eyes, and the children sat either on the ground or on small creepies. Three legs were essential for balance because the uneven ground would easily topple a four-legged seat. In more recent times when four-legged seats took over in the home, the three-legged stool found a home in the cow byre.

Regional styles were known, even with something as simple as the three-legged stool. Once the smoke was brought out through a chimney, the legs were raised on the creepie, but not always to the same height. The seats were generally disc-like, sometimes with the tops of the legs showing through, but more often without. And one particular stool had a hole in the centre, which didn't exactly detract from its purpose as a seat but did have an advantage when one was carrying it. It was rare, even in more recent times, to find a painted stool, and varnished ones were even less common. Generally a good scrubbing was enough.

The seat of honour in the kitchen was determined not by the quality or size of the seat, but by its location. Proximity to the hearth was important, and the grandfather reigned supreme whilst he was still alive. I can remember seeing my own grandfather relaxing in his favourite seat by the hearth, listening quietly and idly poking in the ashes with his stick. However, when visitors arrived, he politely relinquished his seat and moved to a less comfortable form on the other side of the fire.

The settle-bed (*leaba shuidheacháin*) was a marvellous piece of

furniture. Known as the saddle-bed or
just plain settle, its exact origins in this
country are open to doubt. Most historians agree that it probably came
to the farmhouse directly from the
medieval castle kitchens. During the

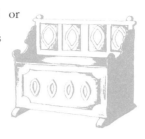

day, it was a box-like seat, but when an extra bed was required at
night it could accommodate up to eight people, depending on size.
In the larger farmhouses, a matching pair was usual, one on each side
of the big hearth. These matching sets invariably displayed a good
deal of ornamentation, and it was not
unusual to find the occasional speci-
men smothered in rich carvings and
panelling.

Rectangular boarded stools known
as forms (pronounced 'furrums'
in country areas; *formaí* in Irish) were popular in the midlands.
Ladderback chairs were also common, and were little more than four-
legged stools with backs, and again they were often home-made. The
wooden seats were soon superseded by plaited
súgán seats, usually woven from twisted straw,
and *súgán* armchairs were often made to match,

though quite often such armchairs were kept in the parlour because of their propensity for coming undone when
not properly woven.

The Windsor chair is perhaps the classic 'cottage' chair,
and the variety that has appeared since its introduction
during the late seventeen hundreds is almost unbelievable. Essentially they were chairs whose turned legs, arm supports, backsticks
and stays were all socketed into the seat, and although there were
dozens of different types of Windsor, they were all distinguishable
as Windsors.

The Windsor chair is an old European type, also very popular in
England where a total of five different craftsmen had a hand in the
production of the one chair. Each had his own title – the benchman did the sawing and fretwork, the bottomer scooped out the
saddle-seats with his long-handled adze, the bender put the final
shape on the pieces sawn by the benchman, the framer assembled the
pieces, and the finisher smoothed it off. A good craftsman could copy
the Windsor style, and although some of the better ones were
obviously originals from England, many of the Windsors
which we see in old farmhouses were made by Irish
craftsmen. The ladderbacks were an older type and
much more common in Ireland.

The different types of Windsor had different

names, most of which were determined by the backrest and how it had been put in. There were combbacks, fanbacks, scrollbacks, archbacks, bowbacks, wheelbacks and arrowbacks. There were dining-chairs, armchairs and handsome rocking-chairs, and because of their strength and lasting qualities many of them have survived to this very day and are still in everyday use. Elm wood was invariably used in the construction of the seat, the legs were turned from beech and any remaining parts were fashioned from yew. A finish of varnish was common, though plain well-scrubbed chairs were preferred in farmhouses where varnish wouldn't survive very long.

Enterprising farmers who didn't go in for 'those new fangled things' sometimes fashioned dugout seats from logs chopped down on their own land. Such seats lasted a long time, just as dugout boats were famous for their durability. Stools and other pieces of furniture were also built in this way when money for 'proper' seating wasn't available. A plaited stool known as a boss was popular in the southeast where boss-making, or lip-work as it was more commonly known, flourished as a craft. Some of the bosses were fashioned only from straw, but a stronger, more long-lasting variety incorporated strips of bramble.

Right top to bottom: low child's chair; child's feeding chair; tall-backed commode chair

Left: typical country dresser

The kitchen dresser, sometimes known as the Welsh dresser because it is believed to have originated in Wales, was a feature of most farmhouse kitchens. It was the housewife's showcase, wherein she displayed her crockery, her willow-pattern delph, her well-scrubbed noggins and piggins and a collection of ornaments and souvenirs given to her by her relatives or family. And if the dresser had a very wide lip at the front, it served as a place on which to lay out a corpse in the event of a death in the family. The traditional dresser had four or five shelves rising above a closed or open cupboard. There were a great many variations because each dresser was made to individual specifications. Some dressers were as wide as ten feet, taking up virtually an entire length of wall, while others were as narrow as three feet. Drawers were fitted in later specimens, and the cupboard space was generally closed. A lot of the household trumpery was kept in this space, away from curious eyes; or, in the case of a meticulous housewife, the pots and pans.

In its earlier form, the dresser was a chunky sideboard on which servants 'dressed' food just before serving. In the medieval kitchens, the Welsh dresser – the sideboard and shelves combined – carried fantastic displays of copper pots, pewterware or silverware. A variation had no cupboard space beneath and no supporting boards behind the shelves.

Right: food-ark

The meal-ark was another important piece of kitchen furniture. It was made by the local arkwright or sometimes by the farmer himself, and was used as a store for flour, bran, brown meal and any other grain product used in the kitchen. Usually there were two compartments, one for white flour and the other for brown meal. The Welsh-ark, known as a coffer in Wales, was introduced to Irish farmhouse kitchens where it became known as the bolting-hutch. It was designed to hold only one foodstuff, and for this reason was not favoured by housewives who used both flour and brown meal daily when baking. My own grandmother had a meal-bin – a two-compartment ark with one lid – but there were also drawer-chests which served the same purpose.

The parlour was undoubtedly for display and little else. When important visitors came to the house – such as the parish priest or local big-shot – they were ushered into the parlour with due ceremony and offered a seat in the cold, musty room, even in wintertime when they would have preferred the warmth and homeliness of the kitchen.

The parlour invariably housed a treasure of quality furniture, as well as the best oil lamp, a well-polished wooden floor, a huge sideboard decked with clutter and organised chaos, and myriad family photographs (when photography became a part of Irish life in the early 1900s). Lace antimacassars adorned chintz-covered armchairs and possibly a fine Windsor rocking-chair, a grandfather clock probably ticked solemnly in the corner, and heavy drapes hung at the window. But for all that, a mustiness permeated the room and the grate lay empty in its classy fire surround, except at Christmastime or on other special occasions when the room would be filled with smoke for hours after the fire was lit. Of course, the musty odour was sometimes overwhelmed by the spicy aroma of furniture polish and floor wax.

Essentially, the parlour was a feature of the farmhouse and not the average labourer's home, and in the majority of cases it was modelled on one of the rooms in the 'big house' or perhaps on the living-room in the local priest's house. It was a luxury beyond the means of many a pocket, but nevertheless a part of our vernacular architecture.

Clockmaking had been established in Europe since the fourteenth century, but during the 1800s new industrial techniques led to the production of cheap wall clocks which found their way into many farmhouses. However, despite their cheapness and reliability, they did not supersede the grandfather clock, many of which dated back to 1600. The grandfather reigned as king of clocks right into this century and was often extremely ornate, displaying lavish marquetry. A plain grandfather was usually more than the average small farmer could afford, so they might have had to content

Left: grandfather clock

themselves with a Dutch clock. This was the most basic chronometer available, consisting of no more than a white face with painted dials and a spray or two of colourful flowers, with an unprotected pendulum and chain weights.

Grandfather clocks were rarely taller than seven-and-a-half feet (2.5m). Sometimes they were even shorter, to fit in under low ceilings. The case was generally made from oak, but some unscrupulous clock-makers stained their oak clock-cases with cow's blood to achieve the reddish sheen of 'mahogany'. These clocks had a dark face with enamel dials. Many were thirty-hour clocks, but eight-day grand-father clocks were known.

The farmhouse bedroom was a spartan affair, often housing little more than a bed or two, a clothes-chest and a table for the night candle. In latter times, a washstand, complete with basin, jug and 'po' or chamberpot, was added in deference to modern hygiene demands.

Beds varied considerably in structure and design, from a basic wooden box with a sack-covered hay mattress in the poorest houses to four-posters in the big farmhouses. My grandparents and many of their contemporaries relied on brass bedsteads in the two bedrooms

Right top to bottom: swing cradle; carved and turned wooden cradle; woven 'Moses' cradle

Right: truckle-bed, designed to be pushed away
under a conventional bed when not in use

and a settle-bed in the kitchen, while my father could remember being banished to the loft when visitors were staying overnight. A sojourn in the loft was, I gather, an eerie experience and one my father and his brother – who usually shared the experience – didn't relish.

Some of the earliest records show that whole families slept on woven rush mats on the floor of early one-roomed houses, barely feet from the animals. In Donegal, it was traditional for the whole family to sleep together in one huge wooden bed, known in some areas as the thorough bed. In damp areas liable to periodic flooding, this bed became known as a truckle-bed because the frame was raised to a safe height on truckles. Later, when a more conventional bed was introduced, the truckle-bed fitted neatly underneath.

The press-bed was a bed which looked for all the world like a cupboard during the day, but which could be used very effectively as a bed during the night. Known in some parts of the country as box-beds, they provided privacy in a crowded room if one of the family

Below left: press-bed; right: large press-bed with fold-away base in use

was feeling ill or peeved and needed to be alone.

The tester-bed is believed to have a longer history. It had a canopy but no sides, and was often low enough to fit in the loft, although getting it there was undoubtedly something of a challenge!

And finally there was the 'outshot' bed or bed-an-nexe, which was peculiar to the kitchens of the north-west, although it was known elsewhere. Generally it was located on the wall adjacent to the hearth, and was sometimes referred to as the 'hag'. Two people could sleep comfortably in an outshot, but as the family grew older, and one of the grandparents perhaps grew infirm, the outshot was reserved for the ailing grandparent.

Returning once more to the kitchen, I would like to mention a few not-so-common pieces, such as a food-cupboard, for instance, used instead of the ubiquitous dresser in some eastern farmhouses. Consisting of closed or louvre-type doors, it was essentially a big press and was probably the forerunner of other pieces of furniture which were modelled on its basic design – the hen-coop, for example, once an important feature of the southwest kitchen, and the meat-safe, whose louvred or wire-mesh doors allowed just enough air in to keep the meat reasonably fresh, whilst keeping flies out.

Holders and racks were popular in farmhouse kitchens and began to be used by poorer households from the early twentieth century

HOME-MADE THINGS

Many of the things made in the farming households of old may seem primitive by modern standards, but they served their purpose adequately, and often there wasn't anything to compare them with in any case. All kinds of materials were worked into containers or tools, especially pliable materials, which could be moulded, and wood. The tools that the farmer used for making things were invariably smith-made and simple, and occasionally a particularly gifted person could produce a work of art using very few tools.

Burden ropes were made and used for transporting small loads, such as a *brosna* of sticks or fodder. Larger loads, or loads of turf and finely cut fodder which couldn't be carried by rope, were carried in *ciseáin* or wickerwork baskets. Some of these baskets had straps or strings for the shoulders.

Burden ropes were fashioned from all kinds of material – straw (for lightweights), hay, strands of tree bark and even seaweed. I can remember seeing my grandmother bringing home on her back rotting sticks she'd collected for the fire, using a modern rope in the old way. Just as ancient as the burden rope for the back was the *fáinnín* for the head. This was a ring of hay placed on the

Left: Basket-maker, Co. Galway
Right: *fáinnín* for head to help balance a load

crown of the head to support considerable burdens, such as a basket of laundry or turf.

Coastal people collected a lot of seaweed for making kelp, for manuring their infertile land and sometimes for food. And in the case of some islanders they had no carts or other large transporter to bring home a heavy load at a time, so they collected smaller loads in back-baskets, or in a pair of creels strapped to a donkey's back. On Aran, a sheepskin was tied to a person's back with a rope knotted at the front before the back-basket was fitted. When using creels the animal's back had to be protected too from the abrasive action of the hard wickerwork. Back-pads were made from straw or hay, or even from rushes. The pad was like a mat draped across the animal's back, and onto it was placed the straddle from which pins projected to take the handles of the creels. Tin panniers could also be attached, or wooden carrier boxes. I've seen good examples of pads and straddles in Knock Folk Museum.

The back-pad and straddle were sometimes joined together. Sometimes called the *cruit* (which means 'hump on the back'), the combined pad and straddle were easy to put on. There were two types of straddle: the crook straddle and the split straddle. They each consisted of a pair of flat boards resting on a straw or hay mat as outlined above. The crook straddle had

(a)   (b)

Above: back-pannier; left: creel-carrying straddle for donkey (a and b indicate hooks for creel support)

only one pair of boards from which hooks projected, the split straddle had two pairs, one smaller than the other. Osier (willow) ties reinforced the bridge between the larger ones, and in Kerry osier loops were sometimes used instead of creel hooks.

A belly-band held the straddle in position, with a supporting crupper running under the tail. A breast-band was added to the harness to balance the weight on the body when heavy burdens such as turf or hay were being transported. Straw ropes generally sufficed as belly-bands and cruppers, but, if possible, the breast-band was fashioned from something stronger, such as leather. A simple bridle of twisted straw completed the harness.

Baskets were known by many different names, depending on their size and on the locality. A large basket was generally a *cliabh*, a fishing basket for holding nets was known as a *caitéog* in Antrim, and as a *ciseán* on the western seaboard. A *ciseog* was a shallow round basket, the type used for holding the potatoes on the table during mealtime and sometimes incorporating a small cup in the centre for salt. A *cleibhín* was a small basket, about the size of a modern breadbasket, and a *caitéog*, as well as being a fishing basket in Antrim and a straw-rope, was also a plaited hen's nest and the name for the rush mats put on clay floors in the old days. In County Clare, any basket was referred to

Above: straw straddle; right: belly-band

as a *lod*, and a *pana ciseán* was a badly made basket, whereas a *cis* was a well-made wickerwork basket.

Basket-making is one of the oldest crafts in the world and it is still a popular craft today. However, nowadays we weave wicker baskets for ornamentation in the home, whereas in the past basket-making was a necessity. Many farmers had their own sally garden behind the house, and when the sallies were ready for harvesting they were cut and arranged in bundles for private use or for sale on fair day.

The materials used in basket-making included raffia (imported), cane (imported), willow, reed, rushes and sally, whilst rudimentary containers were woven from straw and hay. Basket-making with sallies and willows was largely a male occupation because the work was hard on both skin and muscles. Adequate skill was acquired in less than a year by a youngster, and by the time he was in his thirties or forties and had a discerning eye, he could fashion a basket from memory using intricate work.

Two special baskets which required complicated work were the potato-skib, which was a wickerwork strainer (superseded by the colander) and the *sciathóg*, which was a special potato basket for holding potatoes in the field during sowing. (A *sciathóg* was also the name given to the detachable base of a creel.)

The basket-maker who lent himself to all types of basket-making needed to have a good selection of tools. A sharp billhook or knife was used for cutting and trimming, and various awls and bodkins for making holes. A small shears of some kind was used for nipping larger sticks. A good basket-maker cut and prepared his own rods, usually in the autumn when the crisp golden leaves were already shed. The rods were left for several weeks to season, then the rough-work rods were separated from those suited to fine weaving. The latter were stripped of their bark and soaked in hot  water. They were naturally soft grey in colour, but could be dyed in various shades so that interesting effects could be achieved in the pattern. A well-dyed rod is said to have lasted for years without fading.

With willow, the basket-maker had natural brown, natural fawn and natural white to choose from. They were not placed in water, but instead were stood upright against a wall or hedge, once the bark had been stripped off, so that the damp stickiness could dry naturally.

The basket-maker usually worked sitting on a low plank of wood made of elm, measuring three feet in length and two in width.  It was raised a little above the ground at the back end and had a makeshift seat for comfort. The rods lay in a pile beside the craftsman as he worked. A special 'horse' – a sort of plank on legs that was straddled just as if riding a horse – was used by craftsmen who made spale baskets (originally from Wiltshire, England) and trugs (of Lancashire origin). The bushel-trug was particularly useful for carrying potatoes and other produce on the land.

Right top to bottom: turf basket; net basket; spale basket

Above left and centre: mussel traps; right: lobster pot

Nets and ropes – both thick straw *súgáns* and thin twines of twisted yarns – were an important part of daily life. Snared rabbits, for instance, were often brought home in nets, thatched roofs were covered with netting to keep the birds away, onions were stored in nets in wintertime and nets were essential for fishing. Ropes tied down loads, carried loads as burden-ropes, held flapping trouser legs against the legs and were moulded into makeshift baskets and mats. Net-making was a skill known to all coastal fishermen. Certain knots were known: the sheet-bend, double sheet-bend and reef knot. Fishermen generally used only the first of these, using a thick needle and a 'lace', which was a short piece of wood. Not unlike hand-knitting, hand-netting followed moves such as casting-on and casting-off. The fibre used was sisal or hemp-twine.

Straw was woven into *súgán* seats, mats and various types of lightweight baskets. The craft of straw-weaving was known as lip-work. Straw plait was worked into hats, carrier-bags, and even door-panels when wood wasn't available locally. Originally, whole straws were used, but it was discovered that straw which was split gave a neater finish and also went further. Thraw-hooks and scud-winders

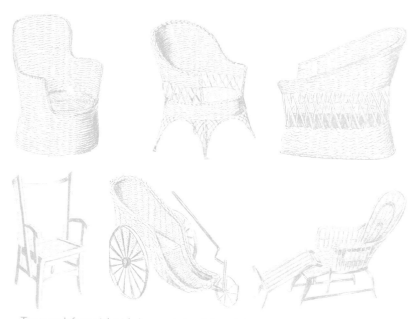

Top row, left to right: *súgán* armchair, wicker chair;
woven wicker armchair for parlour
Second row, left to right: cane seat, invalid's chair, rest chair

were used to make the ropes. They were then twisted tightly in the direction the craftsmen desired until the object was complete.

One important use for straw was as a filler for horse-collars. On page 86, I have shown a whole straw collar, the type used originally without any covering. A piece of cloth was draped over the animal's neck before the collar was put on so as to avoid irritation to the animal's skin. Because of the wear and tear it was subjected to in the course of a day's work, the collar had to be replaced every so often. This meant that the farmer had to be proficient at making replacements as required.

Hens' nests were invariably fashioned from straw or rushes. The nesting basket was always an attractive piece of workmanship and was, apparently, made comfortable for more than economic reasons. Our ancestors, it would seem, believed that when the hens were squabbling amongst themselves at night before settling on their roosts, they were plotting to fly away from Ireland. A comfortable nesting place and a warm hen house were provided as a lure to keep them at home!

Different types of nesting basket were known in different parts of the country. In the midlands the hens had to be content with wooden boxes lined with hay, and although they obliged the farmer's wife by laying in the carefully prepared boxes most of the time, they often wandered off in search of a sheltered bit of hedge or a convenient cavity in the hay-filled manger and laid their eggs there. The housewife always had to have her ear cocked for the sound of cackling from somewhere other than the hen house.

In parts of the southwest, county Limerick in particular, two- or three-tiered chicken-coops were the

Left top to bottom: straw collar with wooden frame; two-storey nesting box; single nesting basket.

order of the day in most farmhouse kitchens; sometimes they were incorporated into the dresser. The coop was vacated and cleaned out during the day, and had fresh hay put in for the night when the hens were brought in from their farmyard wanderings. The coop was fashioned from wood, with a slatted door at the front. A good example may be seen in Bunratty Folk Park in County Clare.

In parts of the west and far south the nesting basket was suspended from a pole in the kitchen; sometimes as many as three or four separate nesting baskets were provided, with the pole from which they were suspended serving as a roost at night. The alternative to a set of individual nesting baskets was a basket-box containing up to four or even six nesting compartments.

For tool-making, wood was widely utilised in the midlands, east and south where it was easily acquired. The most basic of kitchen tools, such as pounding-mallets and beetles, were fashioned from a single length of solid wood. The potato-pounding beetle was an important kitchen tool where animals were fed boiled potatoes. In some kitchens there was a hollow in the flag floor into which the freshly boiled cauldron of spuds was placed direct from the crane. The hole held it secure whilst the contents were being pounded by the long-handled beetle. A mell was a home-made mallet used

Above: hanging nesting basket; right: beetle

87

for pounding whins for the horses, and a similar kind of mallet was used for tenderising meat.

Wood was also used for making tray-type carriers, and for the frames of riddles and sieves. A piece of fine mesh and some small nails were all that was required to complete a home-made sieve.

Coiled food baskets were widely used on the Aran Islands for transporting perishables or for holding food in the home. They had handles and resembled modern buckets. Calf-muzzles or calf-baskets were also woven, usually from rushes, and placed on the calf's head, covering the mouth.

Both pliable materials and wood were used by parents and children to make toys. A child adept at simple weaving could make a little basket for carrying nuts or fruit gathered in autumn. Children often made themselves 'pinkeen' nets for fishing in the local stream, or butterfly cages. And it wasn't unusual in my grandmother's day for a young girl to weave herself a straw or rush hat and decorate it with a daisy-chain or garland of wild roses. The results of her efforts might not have been professional, but at least she derived infinite pleasure from making it herself.

Certain calendar events necessitated the making of ceremonial 'toys' and associated dress. My father remembered receiving a few sticks of 'Peggy's leg', the ubiquitous lucky bag, an

Left top to bottom: riddle; muzzle for calf; baby's rattle

orange, a whistle or bugle, and some mechanical toy or other in his stocking, hung at the end of the bed on Christmas Eve. But prior to that, parents probably fashioned toys from wood or rushes and gave them to the children at Christmastime. I'm sure many a mother was delighted to dress her children up on St Stephen's Day and send them out to 'follow the wran'. The children invariably disguised themselves much as they do today, but the emphasis was on fun rather than on making money. They went to the trouble of seeking out a wren, of sacrificing it and suspending it from a bush; then they carried it from house to house chanting the words of the song:

The wren, the wren,
The king of all birds,
St Stephen's Day was caught in the furze;
Up with the kettle, and down with the pan,
Give me a penny to bury the wran.

Everybody contributed towards the burial. The money didn't, however, find its way inevitably into the children's pockets, but was handed over at the end of the day to provide the drink and food for the evening's festivities. In some parts of the country, straw-boys arrived at the local centre of the night's activity, though they generally appeared only at weddings in many areas. They were known as straw-boys because of their outfits, which were made entirely from straw. In the Dingle area of County Kerry, a *sor sop*, or 'Sir Wisp', was a personage in the wren play and was traditionally clad in a straw suit, masked and armed with a wooden sword or a pig's bladder fastened to a rod. He represented an Englishman, and was defeated in a combat by an Irish 'knight', similarly clad, and known as *Seán Scot*. The spectacle they put on was probably a great source of entertainment for youngsters.

Hallowe'en masks were known in the old days as vizards, and were made and worn by children, as were crosses. The children made their own masks and crosses and used blood, grass and soot to add colour to plain paper or cloth. On St Patrick's Day, special badges, also shaped as crosses, were made, and again home-dyeing was used. Earlier in the year, on the feast of St Brigid, St Brigid's crosses were woven from rushes and worn by girls, along with special belts. And, of course, all young teenage girls knew how to make the four-legged crosses shown here. The *brídeog* was an effigy of the saint, fashioned from old pieces of material and stuffed with straw or hay. A bonnet gave an appearance of reality to the head. The *brídeog* was mounted on a stick and carried from house to house by the leader of the St Brigid's Day procession, usually a young girl.

Above: St Brigid's crosses

Games in rural Ireland consisted mainly of hurling, sling-shooting, football, and in my part of the country skittles was very popular. The Irish country folk were adept at amusing themselves, and *cluiche caointe* was the name used to describe the games people played at funeral wakes. These were often played in the form of pranks, with the least intelligent members of the group being made the butt of the jokes!

THE LAND

When landlordism was abolished in Ireland, we became a nation of small farmers, with each tiny parcel of land standing as an independent unit within the community. Nowadays many of these original farms have been merged to make bigger farms, and consequently many field boundaries have been obliterated from the landscape. When I was a child, my grandparents had a total acreage of something under twenty acres, and that was considered a decent farm then. In more recent times, my own father's eighty or so acres seemed meagre; if my grandfather had had that much land he would have been the local squire!

THE GEOGRAPHY OF THE LAND

The farmhouse, the yard and the outhouses formed the nucleus of the farm, with the land stretching away on all sides. Sometimes the farm was broken up and spread out within a townland or even within a few townlands, and usually the bog was located well away from the main

Left: Ploughing in Co. Dublin
Above: wooden field gate

farm. *Bothairíns* (boreens) linked various fields and plots of ground, and the Mass path linked an entire townland with the local church.

The farmyard was a feature of lowland farms. It was a centre of activity, where the horse was yoked, the hens fed, the farm food-stuffs prepared and the corn threshed. It was central to everything, located as it was like a courtyard amongst the sheds and farmhouse. My grandparents' farmyard was typical of others in the midlands. It ran the length of the thatched house, had sheds opening onto it from two other sides, and a wall running the length of the third side, with the twin stone piers and iron gate smack in the centre of it. A dungheap (*carn*), which was carted out as manure to the land once a year in springtime, was located within sight of the settle-bed where my grandfather normally sat; the dungheap represented what little wealth he had, so he liked to be able to see it when he was relaxing. The yard cockerel greeted the morning from the summit of the heap, his loud raucous cheer echoing for miles, and the hens found it a convenient source of food.

Sheds and outhouses varied from region to region. In the midlands and east, where farmers were marginally more well-off than their western or southern counterparts, the number of sheds was greater on each farm. My grandfather, for example, had a pig-house, a shed for the ass, a barn which doubled as a cartshed, a cow byre for four animals and a couple of sheds for calves of varying ages. The hens, too, had to be housed, as well as the turkeys and geese. Originally, makeshift shelters sufficed, but during my childhood proper sheds were provided. However, the more sheds a farmer had, the more cleaning out he had to do, and although my grandfather was a placid, unconcerned sort of individual to talk to, he was as fastidious as the next man about keeping his farmyard and sheds clean and airy.

The sheds were generally built from wattle-and-daub, or wattle on its own, except in the coastal areas where stone was used for building everything. And where the farm was devoid of decent cover for animals, small huts were built in the bog or elsewhere. In mountainous areas, fox-resistant stone was used to build hen houses, and in parts of the east and mid-lands, brick was used in the construction of pigsties which incorporated pig 'runs'. Cow byres were always low and dark. Wooden or clay partitions separated the cows during milking and a cobbled channel took the urine away to a shore outside the building. Hefty chains attached to the wall above the mangers were tied around the cows' necks to prevent them from wandering. In wintertime, the cows were confined to the cow-shed throughout the day in particularly inclement weather.

Hen houses varied from small makeshift huts accessible to the fox, to big, well-built, airy buildings with plenty of nesting space and roosting poles. Hens, however, are inclined to be independent and often lay their eggs anywhere

Above: lean-to added to dwelling house to store turf; right: hen house constructed from stone with thatched roof

except where they should. A deserted manger, a sheltered spot in the garden hedge or amongst bulky sacks in the barn were all good places to look when eggs weren't appearing in the nests.

Turkeys, when bred by the farmer, were housed separately from the hens, and the geese and ducks were usually housed together in a small shed opening off the farmyard. My own strongest recollection of my grandmother's geese was of the big noisy gander taking after me if I stepped onto his territory. He was the menace of visitors, hissing and honking in a threatening fashion, and because he saw the lough (the small lake in front of the house) as part of his territory, he acted like a watchdog when anyone so much as ventured round the corner of the road. Consequently, my grandmother always knew when a visitor was coming.

The (corn)barn-cum-cartshed had either wide doors which opened out or no doors at all. A loft, which provided extra storage space, was a wonderland of delight for imaginative children, who played there in bad weather. The farmyard gateway was usually dignified by a pair of massive piers, either square or pyramidal, with rounded or conical caps. The farmer was proud of the entrance, and come springtime the house-proud farmer spent some time whitewashing the piers and painting the gate.

Field gates were often unique, with no two in a townland looking exactly the same. Wooden ones were usually home-made and would resemble no other gate anyway, but even the smith-made gates followed no standard pattern, although there was an accepted method of installation. They had to swing forward like a fire-crane, directly on the heel, on a projecting iron spud which swivelled in a stone socket. The handle was simply drawn into a slit in the pier and couldn't be locked as such; a tightly drawn chain could be used to secure it in the closed position. But field gates were often no more than a 'stick-in-the-gap' (*stopallán*), consisting of a heavy pole which was drawn across an open gap at a height considered resistant to animals. When barbed wire became freely available to farmers, they invariably used it to make improvised field gates, as well as strong resistible fences.

The haggard was the storing place for hayricks and cornstacks, and was generally located on high ground behind the house and farm-yard, and was reached by a cart-track from the yard. In flat country, platforms would have to be built for the ricks and stacks, otherwise flooding could undermine them. Another feature of the farmstead in the old days, and located close to the haggard – often beside it – was the kitchen garden, where produce for the table was grown. Traditional cottage herbs were important for flavouring plain food, fruit bushes produced the raw ingredients for jams and chutneys, and fruit trees provided edible delights for the children.

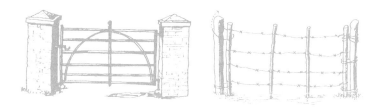

Above left: smith-made iron gate hung between square stone piers; right: barbed-wire field gate

Crops were separated from the animals in the fields by field barriers, usually referred to as ditches. A hedged ditch (*fál*) consisted of a barrier of earth faced on one side with large stones. Hawthorn and bramble were encouraged to grow through the cracks between the stones to form vigorous thickets and render the barrier stock-proof. The double ditch was a feature of my own part of the country. It boasted a width of at least ten feet (3m) and was often as tall as eight feet (over 2m). The path running its length was used by pedestrians in times of flood, and was a favourite route to the fair with animals because the double ditch recognised no townland barriers.

In the west and south, stone was the obvious material when it came to constructing barriers. Stone walls of varying density and design criss-crossed the western counties in a network of effective barriers, and on the Aran Islands stone gates were known as well, although the word 'gates' is probably erroneous in this context because there wasn't, strictly speaking, any gate at all – part of the wall could be dismantled and rebuilt again as required. The other stones in the walls were also arranged loosely so that cows or sheep wouldn't dare touch them for fear of bringing the whole wall toppling down on top of themselves.

The stone barrier associated almost exclusively with County Galway was the dry stone wall similar to the Scots Galloway dyke.

The lower half was constructed from overhanging boulders. In County

Above: slipe for transporting stones, turf, etc.

Clare, Liscannor stone was used in precision-built walls as well as in the more haphazard constructions, and the large flat slabs of grey, slate-like stones were used for roofing as well. Stone barriers also had their own features such as the sheep's pass, which was a small hole in the wall, just high and wide enough to let sheep pass from field to field whilst keeping the other, bigger animals confined to one field. A keeping-hole was a nook in a wall with a slab or wooden base, and it was used for storing large pots, and so on. A similar nook was used for housing one or more beeskeps.

The wayside stile was a feature of the east and midlands and parts of the country where barriers lacked gates in any quantity. A well-trampled path led to and from the stile. The stile itself, whilst on one person's land, was essentially a right-of-way, and there might have been as many as twenty stiles in one townland – each one, of course, occupied by a banshee or spirit of some kind once the witching hour arrived at night! The stile was also a traditional meeting

Right top to bottom: wooden stile; squeezy stile; haggard stile; zigzag wooden stile

Left: zigzag field stile

point for courting couples during the early part of the night.

There were different kinds of stile. The latch-gate stile was familiar at the entrance to churches and churchyards, but wooden and stone stiles were more familiar on farmland. And with the advent of barbed wire, wire stiles were used in haggards and on wire fences. Ladder stiles were often used where fences were particularly high, such as with the double-ditch barrier of the midlands.

Townlands were usually defined by rivers or streams, especially in lowland areas. Spanning the rivers at certain points were 'kishes', or footbridges (*droichead coise*). Most of the kishes were only a single plank in width, but when the river separated one part of a farm from another, the kish would have had to be wide enough to take a cart. A series of planks tied together, raft-like, formed this kind of kish, and two handrails of rope bordered it on each side.

The bog road was a feature of peaty country, where it often swept across the landscape like a primitive highway, for it was frequently high above ground level to avoid flooding. It was a lonely road, and usually a fairly long and straight one, and although used on and off at all times of the year by pedestrians, it didn't come alive until the autumn when the farmers carted their harvest of turf from the bog to the farmyard.

The well, especially the holy well, was a very important feature

of the rural landscape. The ordinary well was often the only source of drinkable water for miles, and if it were believed that it had once been visited by a saint and was, therefore, declared a holy well, all the better, because holy wells were known to carry valuable 'cures'. A few of the more important holy wells were used as shrines, and woe betide the man or woman who used the water for domestic purposes! Any water taken from a shrine was 'blessed' and could be used only as a cure or for sprinkling around the house to keep away evil. On Pattern Day, crowds of country people congregated at the nearest shrine to pray, using notched prayer sticks.

In more recent times ordinary wells were often topped by a draw-well with a rope and crook for the bucket, or by a mechanical pump. The village pump became the traditional meeting place for the women of the locality, just as the smithy, or forge, was the traditional meeting place for their menfolk. In country areas, the pumps were sited at the side of the road in their own little concrete platforms with a concrete or stone wall surrounding them on three sides. A hole in one of the walls gave access to the field beyond.

In the west, the soot house was a common feature, and on Achill Island the remains of an old soot house can be seen. Separate from the farm, yet part of it, the soot house was home to the family for

almost six months, when they lit fires day and night to make soot. The soot gathered as smoke lodged in the chimneyless roof, and when spring came around the whole roof was removed and carted to the fields to serve as fertiliser. A new roof was put on for the following winter when the whole soot-making process began again. When visiting the West Highland Folk Museum in Kingussie in Scotland, I was interested to discover that this tradition was also known on the island of Lewis, where the houses were called black houses.

Ireland is criss-crossed with interesting little narrow roads, even in mountainous and boggy areas where one doesn't really expect to find them. The vast majority of these were originally horse-and-cart tracks or pedestrian pathways, which became rights-of-way between townlands and farms. The transport which travelled on these pathways at the turn of the century was rather primitive and undemanding, so it wasn't until the 1940s and 1950s that a lot of them were properly maintained for modern transport.

Getting around wasn't exactly a problem in the old days, if one didn't hope to get too far; certainly, travel beyond the parish one lived in was rare, and beyond the county boundary was out of the question unless one had a good pony and trap. The

Above: field shelter; left bog shelter

only people who really travelled were those hoping to find work, and their search often brought them to America or England. Travelling for pleasure is a relatively modern concept, although shopping trips to Dublin were known in my grand-mother's time. Such a trip would have been the subject of discussion for weeks – not only in the home but also in the local village and in other people's homes, where much speculating was done. Most travelling was done locally, and unless the whole family was travelling or some merchandise was being transported, it was done on foot. I know of a man who thought nothing of walking the fifty miles from central Westmeath to Dublin because he didn't have the fare for the train.

For travelling on the farm, from farmyard to field and so on, the farmer had the donkey and dray or the horse and cart, or the slide-car in earlier times. The slide-car was a sort of large slipe or sledge with shafts. It

Right top to bottom: wooden pre-Famine cart; wooden fairgoing cart with upright laths; basket slide-car; gurry-butt, for use in the farmyard was pulled along with a draw-rope or chains and could transport fair quantities of sticks, sacks, stones or whatever.

However, the lack of wheels meant there was a great strain on the animal pulling it. A cross between the cart and the slide-car was known in my own area. It consisted of a platform about four feet in length and two feet in width, and it had rollers underneath to prevent it from sinking in marshy or boggy terrain.

Block wheels were used as long ago as 400 BC in Ireland – the term 'blockwheel' describes any wooden wheel made from two or

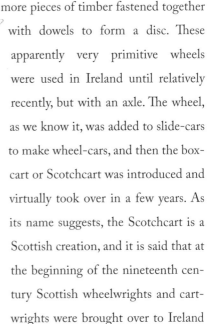

more pieces of timber fastened together with dowels to form a disc. These apparently very primitive wheels were used in Ireland until relatively recently, but with an axle. The wheel, as we know it, was added to slide-cars to make wheel-cars, and then the box-cart or Scotchcart was introduced and virtually took over in a few years. As its name suggests, the Scotchcart is a Scottish creation, and it is said that at the beginning of the nineteenth century Scottish wheelwrights and cart-wrights were brought over to Ireland

Left top to bottom: early Scotchcart; wooden fieldcart; barrow slip

to show Irish cart-makers how to make it. One of its chief advantages was that the sideboards could be removed; they could also be replaced by tall, slatted boards on fairday. When wickerwork sideboards were used, they were known as *ciseáin*.

In the west, the usual driver of a donkey and cart was an elderly woman buried under a black shawl, with a dudeen (pipe) planted in her mouth. A ready tongue and a belt of a thorny stick were enough to control the donkey whenever he became recalcitrant. And if that method of restraint didn't work, she leapt from the vehicle and flung her wool drugget skirt over the unfortunate animal's head!

E.L. Walter, in *The Fascination of Ireland* (London, 1913), mentions the 'pookawn' (*púcán*), which was to be found in Donegal. Fashioned like a Galway hooker, it bore a Spanish-type sail and could be seen 'sailing' about the moorlands of Donegal until the nineteenth century.

A classier mode of transport was the trap, which was used by midland and eastern farmers for family outings. Originally, the trap was designed for the governess, who liked to take her charges out for the occasional trip in the countryside, and it was known as a governess cart. Then, when farmers started using it, it became known as a 'swanky trap' because it seemed infinitely more stylish than the average farmcart. There was seating for at least six – three facing three – and access was through a door at the rear, which dipped down and had a metal step. I can remember being driven to Mass in a neighbour's trap and enjoying myself thoroughly; the fact that it was a fine day may have helped of course, because the trap was open to the elements and could be uncomfortable in wintertime.

One of the most interesting vehicles to travel on the roads in the old days was the gipsy vardo – or caravan, as we refer to it today. Vardos were extremely colourful, and were an intrinsic part of early circuses. Tinkers and Travellers generally travelled in similarly shaped, but less colourful caravans.

Bicycles travelled the roads from about 1900, although the hobby-horse and phantom bicycles were known before then. The boneshaker – an aptly named bicycle if ever there was one – did have pedals, but the rider had to pedal frantically to make even the slowest progress. As for the penny-farthing – its main disadvantage was its high front wheel topped by the saddle; the pedals were also attached to the front wheel, and for a tall man the total diameter of the wheel, which could be five feet (about 1.5m), was determined by his leg length and pedalling method. The diameter of the front wheel of a woman's bicycle was considerably less.

Lighting one's path was important when the roads were rutted and filled with potholes. In 1898 the first acetylene (carbide) lamp was designed for use with the bicycle and did wonders for night cycling. When my father was young and a keen cyclist, he never went anywhere on the bike without his carbide lamp and bicycle clips, a pair of metal open rings which held the flaps of wide trousers neatly against the leg to avoid accidents with the spokes of the wheels. A bicycle pump too was carried at all times because the roughness of the country roads could puncture a tyre, and all cyclists were encouraged to carry a chain-box, some solution and patches for a fast puncture. A few blasts from the pump might be sufficient to keep a slow puncture from hampering travel.

The Sunday Mass and a monthly expedition to the local town for food supplies were often the only outings in a woman's life. In some parts of the country it was traditional to walk to Sunday Mass. Crowds of people would be seen making their way along the Mass path. The children, of course, 'got up to divilmint' by tying *traithníns* of grass together to make foot traps – a childish prank that often had hilarious results!

Above: gipsy vardo

SPRINGTIME ON THE LAND

Traditionally, the feast day of St Brigid, 1 February, marked the beginning of the farming year, and in olden times the farming family assembled in one of the fields to 'turn the sod'. This was an annual ritual accompanied by the reciting of certain prayers. And traditionally, ploughing did not take place until that very important first sod had been turned by the spade. However, in recent times, the ploughing often took place during the wintertime, usually before heavy frost.

THE PLOUGH

From the time of the primitive digging-stick, whether pointed or spade-like, people have tried to speed up the process of tilling the land. One of the earliest foot ploughs known on Irish land was the *cos-chrom* (translated as 'bent foot', meaning that one had to bend over when using it). For centuries, the cumbersome breast plough was used for opening the soil. A misnomer if there ever was one, the

Left: Hand-made turf
Above: removing 'top-dressing' dung from tipcart

Left top to bottom: *cos-chrom* plough; early Irish foot plough; thigh pads worn by user of breast plough; using a breast plough

breast plough was thrust forward with hip or thigh power rather than by the force of chest movements.

In Ireland, the heavy loy plough (from *laí* or *laíghe*) was well known in parts of Cavan and its surrounding counties and in the southwest. It was said that a dozen strong men armed with loys could turn an acre in a day.

Footrests were important on digging implements; sometimes nothing more than a block of wood wedged into a socket at the side of the spade-head, sometimes incorporated into the original design of the piece of metal forming the head, they varied according to local preference. Size and shape of both footrest and digging-head were determined by local conditions, and were standardised in any one area. Swallowtail blades and tapered blades were popular in some areas, whilst straight blades, well sharpened, were the norm elsewhere.

In Mayo, the gowl-gob (from *gabhal-gob*, meaning forked beak) was a curious two-headed spade used in loose sandy soil, where it was said to be ideal for making ridges. The Irish spade differed from the English not only in its narrow bent blade, but also in other respects, such as the way it was put to use – the Irish dig with the right foot, the English with the left!

The early ploughs were primitive implements, even the early versions of the modern plough. With many of the early wooden ploughs used in Ireland an implement called a mattock, or *matóg*, was used to turn the first layer of earth. It was a sort of hoe and was difficult to use over a long period. The first real improvements in the development of the plough occurred in the 1700s, with the first lightweight plough arriving into the British Isles from Holland. However, it was a Scotsman named James Small who invented a plough which one could operate easily, whilst keeping the horses under control, without the assistance of a second person. The first all-iron plough was built in 1800, and since then ploughs of all shapes, sizes and capabilities emerged annually. A trip to any folk museum – the Irish Agricultural Museum at Johnstown Castle in Wexford in particular – will vouch for this. And you will find that no two ploughs are exactly the same, even though there were hundreds of each type made.

There were swing ploughs and wheel ploughs. The turnwrest plough had two blades and was simply turned around at the end

Above: early swing plough

of each furrow to make the return trip using the other blade, and it could be either swing or wheel. Generally, the swing ploughs had no wheels and were popular with small farmers because they were cheap to buy. Because they sometimes had a wooden frame, few have survived.

The multi-furrowed plough was introduced before the end of the 1880s and was a great improvement for the farmer with big acreage, for it meant that he could get a lot of ploughing done in a relatively short time. However, it was a very heavy implement in the early stages of its development and required far too many horses to pull it, and therefore didn't enjoy too much success. The two-furrow plough was much more successful, at least until the advent of steam, when the steam tractors pulled the multi-furrowed plough with considerable ease.

When ploughing for tillage, the most suitable length for a furrow was 220–250 yards, and it was from this that the old division of the mile – the furlong (furrow-in-length) – evolved. The time taken to turn the horses at the ends of the furrows added up significantly, so that in a field with fifty turns to the acre a full thirty minutes or more were taken up with the turning. Two horses were usual, although as many as six were employed where land was particularly heavy. The average speed was two miles per hour. In a day, a man and his horses walked up to eight or nine miles, and in the case of two horses, each one pulled a weight of up to 280lbs.

Steam power in the 1920s brought considerable changes. Following experimentation, it was discovered that the ploughing was a greater success if two machines were used together, which meant that only tillage contractors, as they called themselves, could afford to do steam ploughing. They travelled from farmer to farmer, quickly earning the cost of their new machinery. But it wasn't always a great success; the power of the steam engines drove the plough very deep, sending the valuable top soil too far down, which, in the case of thin soil, was detrimental to subsequent crops.

The success of two engines working together depended on a rapport between the two engine-men, for the only means of communication during a ploughing session was the engine whistle, which they blew loudly in various signals to 'voice' their messages. The whistles didn't carry well on windy days, and this often meant that the work had to stop. A six-furrow plough could work up to fourteen acres in a day, which compared rather well with the one acre ploughed by horsepower.

THE PARTS OF THE PLOUGH

Early ploughs were simple in structure, but the more recent creations were complicated pieces of machinery. The share was the cutting part of the implement, and on early ploughs, which were invariably wooden with only one share, they were known as winding-boards. When iron shares were used, several interchangeable shares were used on the one plough, and their cutting angle could be altered. The coulter (*coltar*) made the vertical cut into the soil immediately in front of the share. Continuing behind the share was the mould-board, which was the most prominent part of the implement.

A wheel could easily be clogged up with clay and be difficult to pull. A sharp object was used to remove the clay; alternatively, a pair of special wheel-scrapers was attached to the plough. A spanner, too, was necessary on occasion and was carried in a special socket. Chain-traces were the chains by which the horses pulled the plough. They were kept clear of the animal's body by means of a crossbar called a whippletree or swingletree, or by the doubletree in the case of two or more horses. These attachments were fashioned from ash wood with iron grips, but special all-iron or all-steel ones were used for very heavy work.

BREAKING UP THE SODS

The earth which was drawn back into furrows by the plough had to be broken up before the seeds could be sown. Clod-breaking implements were fashioned to do this, including extra heavy mallets. However, machines such as grubbers and the cultivator appeared during the early 1900s and did a very efficient job – six acres could be broken up in a single day. A grubbing hoe was a special implement used for this purpose in parts of the west and south.

Left top to bottom: drag board (County Kerry), metal earth-roller, home-made clod-breaking machine

When the clods were broken, a roller was drawn over them to flatten down the earth even more. Rollers varied in design from lightweight wooden ones, which had to be drawn over the ground many times to give decent results, to heavyweight metal 'Cambridge' rollers for extra heavy work with more than one or two horses. The drag-board was used in poorer areas, especially in Kerry and the west.

The harrowing was the next job. This was accomplished with the toothed harrow, which was drawn over the rolled ground to rough it and make it suitable for seeding. Harrows varied from home-made wooden frame harrows with curved wooden or iron tines (teeth), to multiple disc harrows and spring-tooth harrows. Chain harrows were also known, and often came in zigzag patterns for well-dispersed work.

The more advanced harrows were driven, which meant that the operator could control both machine and horses from a bucket-like seat. Like the plough, the primitive harrow is of great antiquity and has appeared in many illuminated manuscripts and in the Bayeux Tapestry of the eleventh century.

Right top: spring harrow; bottom: wooden frame harrow

SOWING THE GRAIN

The next job in the tillage field was the sowing of the grain. I can remember seeing my father hand-sowing from a scooped-up apron held before him. He had never invested in a proper sowing-fiddle,

which was a small machine that sent seed broadcast when the 'bow' was moved over and back rhythmically. The seed was held in a sack inside the seed-box of the machine and a measured amount was released with each movement of the bow, expelling it for anything up to twelve feet (3.5m or so), which meant that less walking was necessary than with the apron or its alternative, the seed-basket or seed-hip. The single-wheel, barrow-like broadcaster was also used; it was wheeled along by hand, its long wooden hopper having apertures on the underside for releasing the seeds evenly, which were sent broadcast by little brushes arranged along the hopper. On big farms, where huge fields were seeded, the horse-drawn broadcaster was used. When in use, the two seed-boxes were arranged in line and the axle and gear wheels at each end provided the

Left top to bottom: sowing-fiddle; seed-hip; seed-box with shoulder strap; using the sowing-fiddle

power for the internal mechanism that sent the seed forth in measured amounts.

The swivel broadcaster was a large, horse-drawn affair, introduced as the 'new, improved' broadcasting machine, and it cost no more than £13 to buy! It had only one seed-box, lined with zinc at the bottom that sent the seeds through to the ground. The box was centred on the main shaft of the vehicle and therefore placed no extra weight on the horse's back. However, some boxes were as wide as sixteen feet (almost 5m), and could not pass through gateways when in the open position. So, to close them, the farmer moved a lever which swivelled them on the main frame and they closed over so that one end was directly behind the horse's tail and the other beyond the main body of the vehicle.

Once the seed was sown, a second harrowing was advisable to roughen up the ground and bury at least half of the grains at a gentle depth below surface level. The roller, or a levelling-box, was then employed to smooth the ground, and a scarecrow (*taibhse*) was erected to keep the crows away. Other crow-scaring devices were introduced, but the *taibhse* was traditional, and was a good way of using old clothes. Clappers, consisting of two boards lightly tied by cords to each side of a third

Above: levelling-box in use; right: the 'new, improved' sowing-machine of the 1800s

board with a handle at the end, were rattled to frighten the crows away; using clappers meant that the farmer or one of his children had to be in the vicinity of the tillage field at all times throughout the day. Nor is the modern 'banger', as we call it locally, a modern phenomenon, as some people might expect. This method of scaring crows was developed as long ago as 1850. My father recalled how one particular 'banger' method worked. In the old days, carbide (acetylene) for the lamps was bought in a tin, but the tin was not discarded when empty. Instead, my grandfather kept it until springtime, when he punctured a hole at the base and placed in it a small piece of grey-white carbide. A drop of water, often some spittle, was aimed at it to rise the acetylene gas, and the lid was secured as tightly as possible. A match was then struck close to the hole, whilst the striker held his head well away. A lid that was too light caused a blaze to shoot forward, but if it were properly secured, a loud bang reverberated around the field and sent the troublesome crows squawking for the nearest cover.

The rook-battery was another creator of noise. It consisted of a circular plate of tin, eighteen inches in diameter, with a strong hoop soldered onto the circumference. Twenty-four or so embrasures were pierced into the hoop, and at each of these a small brass cannon was mounted, and all were loaded with gunpowder. A solution of saltpetre provided the firing power – a

Above: bird-scaring devices

cotton wire was dipped into it and then held onto the touch-hole of each cannon by copper wire attached to the platform. The battery stood in the cornfield on three legs, and was moved regularly so the rooks and other crows wouldn't get used to having the sound come at them from one direction only.

OTHER CROPS

The 'spud', or potato, was the most important root crop and remains so for most of us in rural areas even today. Nowadays we eat Golden Wonders and Kerr's Pinks with relish, but in the old days the popular strains were Epicure, Red Elephant and Champion, whilst Aran Banners were fed to the pigs.

My father planted potatoes just as his father before him did – in lazybeds. These were wide seed-drills separated from each other by narrow trenches. The bank of earth which formed the actual ridge was about three feet (1m) in width (that is, three stalks wide). The seeds, which were cut in half with part of an 'eye' remaining in each half, were sown in March–April, and the young foliage was visible in May. However, the crop wasn't ready for the first harvesting until late July at the earliest.

The dibber, or dibble, was the traditional planting tool. It was used to make holes for the seeds, which were planted

Above: potato-planter; right: single dibber

Left: multiple dibber

directly from a large *ciséan* (basket) one by one. In parts of Cavan and the midlands, the dibber was known as the 'steeveen' (from the Irish, *stibhín*) and was always used by the woman of the house, who was said to be 'guggering' (from *gogaire*, meaning to crouch or bend over – as she would when planting the seeds).

'Earthing-up' or *lánú* of the potatoes was done twice in the course of the following months – three weeks after the actual sowing, and again a month later when the stalks were well out of the ground. In the midlands, the shovel was used to scoop up loose clay from the trench and distribute it over the ridge. In the south and west, the plough was drawn between the ridges, which were traditionally wider there, to break the earth for the same kind of earthing-up. The spraying against blight was done before the blossoms appeared. A solution of bluestone and washing-soda was prepared in the kitchen and taken to the potato field, where the farmer commenced spraying with a besom by dipping it into the solution and jerking it away from him so that liquid was sent broadcast. The smell of blight was often detected in the month of August, but if it were detected earlier, before the crop was yet edible, fear was

Right: beanbarrow

struck into the farmer's heart. In 1845, at the outset of the Great Famine, it was said to have been detected in most areas as early as June.

The turnip was another important rural crop. It was sown in long drills, often running the length of the field alongside the potato ridges. The tiny seeds were treated with red lead prior to sowing, as a guard against birds taking them, and they were sometimes sown with a special seed-hopper or drill. Less well-off farmers had seedbarrows, and the poorest farmers simply sowed by hand. As the crop advanced towards maturity, a lot of weeding was necessary and this too was done by hand, using a hoe of some kind in the early stages and the hands only for the thinning-out stage, when eight out of every ten plants were removed from the drill to allow the remaining two to grow well.

The hand hoe was replaced on the larger farms by horse-drawn hoes, drawn between two rows each time. A pair of tines on each side removed the weeds from the inner edges of the drills, but did not damage the turnip plants. Experience taught the farmer how to gauge the distance between drills when making them in the first place.

THE BOG IN SPRINGTIME

Peatland covered a good percentage of rural Ireland, and in the old days almost every farmer had a *portach*, or bank of peat, to work on in the spring. The bog was a lonely wilderness, whose size was determined by its location. In Donegal, for instance, the bogs and moors seemed to stretch on forever, whereas in the midlands a bog was often a stretch of acid ground running along a river valley, with verdant hills and even buildings visible from its deepest depths. I loved the bog when I was young and have many pleasant memories of hours spent exploring amongst the bulrushes and unusual grasses that lined the fast-flowing freshwater streams criss-crossing it. A variety of sights and sounds indigenous to that particular environment became familiar to me over the years – the goat-like call of the jacksnipe, the lonesome whine of the curlew, the shriek of the otter and the distinctive bark of the fox in the early evening. The most awesome sight has to be 'Jack the Lantern', a huge ball of gas that rises from the ground and floats by in all its glowing glory! The water from the bog streams was always crystal-clear and lovely to drink, and watercress flourished in great abundance.

My grandfather's midland bog produced a dark peat which dried rock-hard, but in other parts of the country the peat remained brown to grey-brown, depending on the type of bog. A bog which was *trom fhódach* was heavy-sodded ground, and a *portach dhá fhód déag* was particularly good because it was 'twelve-sod deep'. When a farmer didn't own a bog of his own, he could lease 'a bit of a digging' from the State. This, of course, was often a risk in damp years because turf needed a 'keen breeze' to dry it for use in the fire.

A whiff of pale-grey turf smoke escaping from where the 'tay' brewed in the old black kettle was often the only indication to the passer-by that the bog was peopled. It was traditional in the old days for a large group of men from an area to work at each man's turf in turn, each one playing host when his turf was being harvested. One season's cutting supplied a family with firing for the year – the black bottom-peat for the winter use, the brown sphagnum peat for the summer use.

When cutting peat, the first stage was the opening up of the bank, which involved the removal of the top layer of tough, fibrous peat, referred to as 'fum'. It made poor firing, but a slipe-load of these parings was a welcome sight to a poor man with no peat of his own. A flatcher was used to remove the parings from the bog; a common garden spade worked equally well in recent times. Soft dry parings were sometimes kept back to be spread out on the cutaway bog below the bank as dry footing.

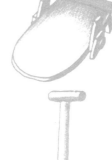

When cutting turf, it was very important for the *sleadóir* (turfcutter) to 'keep a straight face' – that is, to keep a straight face on the bank being worked. A man who couldn't was called a 'clodcutter'

and was derided by his mates. Later, when finishing off, it was customary in some northwestern areas to leave three steps of turf uncut. This was to avoid the curse of St Colmcille, who was once trapped in

Right top to bottom: boot fitted with digging 'foot'; digging 'foot'; mud spade a boghole and subsequently put a curse on any turfcutter who didn't leave a way out of the hole.

The traditional turfcutting implement was the slane (also shlawn, from *slén*). Generally, the type of slane used was determined by the type of bog being worked and by the method of turfcutting. Basically, there were two methods – vertical and horizontal – though each farmer had his own favourite way of thrusting the slane or lifting the turves from the bank.

Vertical cutting, or underfooting, was favoured in thin, upland bogs and was difficult work, whereas horizontal cutting, or breasting, was an easier method that was used in lowland bogs. With breasting there was considerably less strain on the back, and the work was fairly fast because the turfcutter put the sods directly from the slane onto the barrow.

Slanes were made to measure and varied quite a bit in size and design. Consisting of four parts – the blade (*iarann*), the spade-tree (*sail*), the shaft (*cos*) and the hilt (*dorn*) – the slane is a very old implement. The breasting implement was distinguished from the underfooting slane by the upward slant of its cutting edge, whereas the wing of the underfooter slanted downwards. Sometimes some tow roots got caught up on the blade and made working difficult.

Left and right: turfcutters and slanes

The bogbarrow was an important means of transportation in the bog. Fashioned from laths of wood (often crudely, and without any wheel at all), it was used to transfer the freshly cut sods of turf from the bank to the drying ground. Sometimes a small slipe was used, especially on wet ground, where it could be pulled along the slithery surface more easily than a barrow would have been wheeled or carried.

The drying of the turf took a long time, especially in wet years. Sometimes the whole harvest was lost, but when it wasn't inclement the sodden turves were removed from the barrow and spread on the *scair* by a spreader, using a turf fork or pike. A week later, following a fairly dry spell, the turves were ready for footing. Six to eight turves were placed against each other in sets of two, more along the top, to form a *coirceog* (cone-shaped mound). The number of *coirceogs* depended on the amount of turf being footed. Footing was generally children's work, done after school or on a fine Saturday, and my father recalled how it used to be when boredom set in as the work became routine towards the end of the session – one remark of an insulting or scathing nature was enough to spark off a session of scraw flinging, which all too easily went beyond the realms of fun. It wasn't unusual for someone to end up in a boghole!

Above: bogbarrow;
right handbarrow

Once the turf was declared 'bone dry' by the farmer, it was built into a large rick and covered with a water-resistant roof of thatch. However, by now the wind should have formed a tough, water-proof skin on the sods and drained them of most of their eighty percent moisture. Once the turf was sufficiently 'seasoned' in the autumn, it was drawn home to the farmyard for storing. A donkey and cart provided the usual transport in the midlands, but in the west and south slide-cars and creels were used for this important end-of-year task.

Right: Potato planting, Ballynagall, Co. Kerry

THE HARVEST

The work period known as the harvest spanned the summer and autumn months, starting with the haymaking and concluding with the Harvest Home festivities. Compared to modern harvesting, it was slow and tedious work in the old days, rushed only when rain was expected; in those days, farmers relied on their knowledge of the countryside and nature as their weather guide.

THE HAYMAKING

Preparation for the haymaking was made as early as February, when the farmer set aside one or more fields for meadow. Then, later in the spring, he set about encouraging the crop to produce a higher yield by spreading farmyard manure on the still pasture-quality grass. This spreading of manure was known as top-dressing, and was accomplished in one of four ways. Firstly, it could be spread as a solid, direct

Left: Men carry bundles of heather/furze, Great Blasket Island, c. 1924
Above: loading up the hay for the journey to the haggard

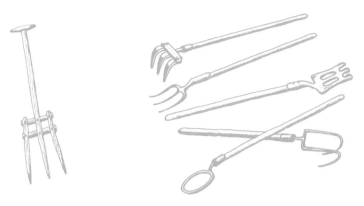

Above left: home-made dowelled dung fork; right top to bottom: dung drag; graip; smith-made dung lifter; two-pronged dung drag; cow-pat lifter

from the dungheap in the yard. The well-to-do farmers often had carts with tilting mechanisms, which made the removal of the dung onto the field a fairly simple process. But I can remember seeing my father using a pitchfork to remove the dung from his cart, a little at a time, until the selected field was dotted with small blackish heaps. Later, it was spread out evenly until the whole field was dressed. Some farmers had a dung drag, a special fork for pulling the dung from the cart onto the ground. And a wooden dung fork, pegged together with dowels, was often used instead of a graip to spread it. In very poor areas, manure-spreading often meant lifting cowpats from one field and putting them on another, using an implement with a circular head.

Liquid fertiliser was sometimes used in preference to solid farm-yard manure. A barrel distributor, mounted on two wheels and drawn by a horse, was used for dispersing the liquid (urine collected over a period of time in the sheds). An early form of muck-spreader, or 'box distributor' as it was called in early catalogues, was used by well-to-do farmers to spread soft slurry manure by spraying it onto the land. The manure fell from a transverse, box-like hopper onto revolving tines, which flung it from the rear of the machine.

The fourth method of manuring land was to fill a seed-hopper with bonemeal and distribute it evenly on the ground, a method used in the east and north when farmyard manure wasn't produced in the amounts required.

Once the meadow was tall enough – usually mid-June – the farmer arranged to have it cut. If he didn't have a scythe or – in recent times – a mowing-machine, he had a neighbour or contractor do the mowing for him. Different types of grasses were known – the *féar caorach* was the sheep's fescue, the *féar capaill* was the timothy grass and the *féar garbh* was the cocksfoot, which produced a particularly coarse type of hay. A bad grass was *féar gaoil*, the quitchgrass. The *féar gorta* was the 'hungry grass', a type of mountain grass bewitched by the fairies, which brought on an unnatural craving for food if one should inadvertently step on it! The 'cure' was a little food – as little as a crumb even – carried on one's person!

Above left: liquid manure-spreader; right: serrated dung knife

When the hay was cut into swaths, it was left to dry for a couple of days, then turned by fork or graip for drying on the other side. It was then shaken out and made into *cociní* (cockeens, cutyeens or lap-cocks) and, unless very dry, left to stand in the field for some days for further drying. Lapcocks varied from rolls like ladies' muffs, through which the wind breezed, to small haycocks. Once fully dry, they were shaken out for a second time and built into proper fieldcocks between seven and eight feet tall. *Súgáns*, or hayropes, were then twisted and drawn over the cocks to secure them. Heavy stone weights at the ends of the ropes held them down in high wind. The farmer usually 'headed' the cocks at this stage too. This was done by raking all the loose hay from the cock to tidy it, then replacing it on top with a pitchfork. The best time for cutting hay was in June when the grasses were in flower; a crop of hay from a June cutting was a prized posses-sion. Also, it left behind a significant 'eddish' (aftergrass).

The mowing-machine was introduced at the turn of the century, but prior to the machine age, the scythe was the traditional hay-cutting implement. And even today it is hard to beat it for mowing awkward gardens and corners of fields. The long-handled scythe has always been favoured by Irish farmers, and because it was built to the farmer's own specifica-tions in the old days, no two

Left above: hand rake;
bottom: paddy rake

scythes were exactly the same.

Basically, the scythe was made up of four important parts – the handle, the handgrips, the blade and the guard.

A smith-made blade was a prized posses-sion, and old blades were never thrown away, but instead were hafted for slicing vegetables or for slicing hard-packed hay from the hag-gard rick, and for a variety of other farmyard cutting jobs. The blade was sharpened with a special honing-stone called a strickle, a job which was repeated several times during a mowing session. The strickle was carried in a leather sheath attached to the farmer's belt, or placed in a special socket on the handle of the implement. An older method of sharpening was with the riff, which was fashioned from wood instead of the more familiar stone, smeared with goose grease at the sharpening end and then sanded. When pulled over the blade in one direction only it acted like a file. Coarse sand was used when a slightly serrated edge for cutting briars or tough weeds was required, fine sand for field work.

The handle of the scythe was called the *crann*, the *snáith* or the sned, depending on the part of the country. The average length was five-and-a-half feet, and a curve was gen-eral, although straight-handled

Above: large hay scythe; right: early mowing-machine

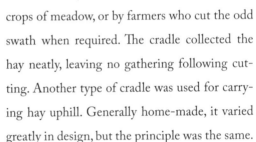

scythes were known in certain areas.

When honing the blade or fixing the handgrips, the farmer held the scythe upright to avoid accidents, for a scythe balanced wrongly could easily topple over and do him an injury. A metal spike at the end of the *crann* usually solved the problem by securing the implement on the ground. The spike was called a grass-nail.

The cradle was a feature of scythes used by farmers with small crops of meadow, or by farmers who cut the odd swath when required. The cradle collected the hay neatly, leaving no gathering following cutting. Another type of cradle was used for carrying hay uphill. Generally home-made, it varied greatly in design, but the principle was the same.

The horse-drawn mowing-machine was a riding machine with a sprung seat and a long draught pole centred between two horses. It travelled on two sizeable landwheels, set wide apart and slatted for better grip. Consisting of three main parts – the truck or carriage (main body), the cutting blade and bar, and the draught-pole and whippletree for attachment to the harness

Left, top to bottom: scythe, with cradle for grass; hay and straw cradle, used for carrying small loads uphill on the back; horse-drawn mowing machine

Right top: straw fork; middle: straw knife

– the mowing-machine was at its best when brand new and with a sharp blade. However, it became sluggish very quickly, so that the blades required constant sharpening and altering.

The actual haymaking didn't really begin until the swaths were on the ground. The hand tools used included the fork, the rake and the four-pronged graip. A variation of the field rake, which was worked by the women, was the drag rake. This was a much larger implement and was always worked by the farmer himself.

Some of the haymaking machinery was dangerous. For instance, the tedding-machine had projecting tines which lay open and

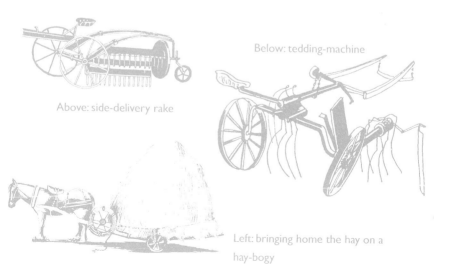

Above: side-delivery rake

Below: tedding-machine

Left: bringing home the hay on a hay-bogy

unprotected on many of the earlier machines; a few had a protective covering of iron sheeting, but accidents involving children occurred all too frequently. The 'tedder' teased the hay into the cocking stage, and a horse-drawn machine rake, known as a dump rake, was then used to bring the hay close to where it was to be built into a cock. Another machine, used in the drying stage, was the swath-turner, which saved a lot of time in the early stages of haymaking. The side-delivery rake sometimes assisted it by drawing every two freshly turned swaths into one windrow.

The fieldcocks stood in the field for anything up to two months, then had to be drawn home to the haggard – the traditional storing place for the crops. The hay was transported to the haggard in fine

autumn weather; the hay-bogy was usually used for this task in the midlands. Other bogys, sometimes called sweeps, were also known. Horse-drawn hay-carts – some with a hayrack fitted – and slide-cars were also used, and in very poor areas a donkey might be seen being led home with a mighty burden of hay on his back.

Some of my clearest childhood memories are of helping my father to bring home the hay. My contribution to the actual work was minimal – mostly because

Left top: barn rope-twister;
middle and bottom: hayrope twisting tools

I kept diverting from our course to help myself
to blackberries which flourished so abundantly
in the hedges – but I remember being given
the job of driving the donkey and hay-filled
cart from the field to the haggard, where my
father added my load to the growing hayrick.

I can also remember helping my father to
make hayropes the old way, using a home-
made winder fashioned from a length of
twisted wire. Sometimes rope-winders were
made from wood and were called thraw-
hooks, or from a mixture of wood and wire
and called scud-winders. The ropes, or *súgáns*
as they were called, were made by feeding

the hay slowly onto the hook of the winder, which was constantly
turned. The *rópadóir* (twister) moved away as the length of the rope
increased. The footrope was the name given to the rope securing a
large haycock.

The hay in the haggard was built into a large rick. Well-to-do
farmers often had special elevators to take the hay up to the rick
as the mound grew. But generally, men on the ground pitched the
hay up to men on the top, and when the rick was made a ladder was

provided. Then the sides of the rick were manicured with a rake, especially at the base, and headed, then secured with strong ropes from which rocks were suspended. Once the cold biting winds of winter came, the hay in the haggard was used as fodder, and was a vital food source for the animals in the fields.

THE GOLDEN HARVEST

The 'Golden Harvest' began with the preparation of the soil and ended with the Harvest Home festival. Strictly speaking, though, it began in August when the ripe corn was golden yellow.

There were four main corn crops: wheat, oats, barley and rye. In the midlands, oats and barley were the main crops, in the east, wheat, in the west and south, oats and barley, and in the north, oats and rye

Below: harvest scene in the field

and also flax, which was a flowering plant grow
as the raw material for the linen industry.

Spring wheat was sown in March, together
with any other cereal crops to be harvested
during the summer. Winter wheat was sown
later in the year. Oats were the most common
crop, mainly because the damp climate suited
them so well and the straw was extremely ver-
satile. However, with oats the harvesting had to
be well gauged because overripe grains invariably
fell to earth and were lost during the cutting. With
all of the cereal crops, such 'lodging' was a risk in stormy weather,
when the wind beat relentlessly at the waving corn and sent some of
it to ground level, rendering it impossible to cut. Badgers and flocks
of birds also had the same damaging effect.

The sickle is one of the oldest surviving implements in farming, and indeed it is still used in areas inaccessible to the reaping-
machine. The design of the sickle is outstanding, because one can use
it for a whole day without feeling unduly tired. Traditionally, women
reaped with the sickle
and men with the heavier
toothed-reaper, a sort of

Right top: mowing-sickle;
middle: corn scythe;
bottom: reaper-binder

sickle but with a heavier blade and serrated edge. The corn was cut by bending over it, grasping a bunch of straw in the left hand, inserting the hook and drawing it towards the body in a sawing action. Gentleness was important if no grain was to be lost from ripe crops. It was also important to cut 'low and clean – to the living earth', as they used to say in the midlands years ago.

Loghter-hooks (from *luchtar*, 'armful') or pick-thanks drew the loghters into sheaves. Resembling a walking-stick, the loghter-hook was a 'tidy' of sorts, keeping the corn neat. A gavel was a similar crooked implement used with barley, whose seedheads were inclined to take up a lot of space and required more control from the reaper.

Once the loghters were bound into sheaves, a few more workers came behind and arranged the sheaves into stooks. In the midlands, stooks were built up in stages, starting with five or six sheaves for the first drying, then ten or twelve, with a head of two sheaves. The tiebands, made with a length of straw deftly twisted away from the sheaf, were loose enough to allow a toe of a boot to fit easily. Too loose and the sheaf would collapse with the least handling.

Wind and sun dried and seasoned the stooks over a period of a few weeks. Fieldstacks then had to be made, which consisted of ten or twelve stooks with their butts out. Various local names were known, such as *adag* (northeast), *stucóg* (west)

Left above: barley gavel; bottom: barley hummeler

and *bart* (south). In my own locality, the midlands, it was called a *síog*, pronounced 'shig'.

When the corn (as all the cereal crops were collectively known), was dry, it was transported to the haggard in large carts. A large rick was built and for that job it was every man who was available! Two kinds of rick were built – the kneestack, made by a man on top and a group of men on the ground pitching up the sheaves, and the overhand stack, made from the ground without a ladder.

The *meitheal* was an important feast associated with the harvest. Originally the word meitheal was the Irish word for a gang of workmen working together with any major crop, but over the centuries it has come to mean 'Harvest Home', the all-important festival at the end of the summer when the harvest was in and the country folk celebrated their prosperity. The feasting at the *meitheal* was shameless, and there were barrels and half-barrels of 'porter' and 'stout', and the odd *cruiscín lán* filled with *póitín* and *uisce beatha*. Dancing and music generally prevailed and the evening was guaranteed to inspire gaiety.

The *meitheal* gradually became a thing of the past when mechanisation shortened the harvesting period. When the reaper-binder appeared, it was received with a mixture of awe and disbelief, for not only could it cut the corn efficiently, but it could also bind it. Speed was improved and in some cases, quality. When the massive combine-harvester appeared on the scene, it did everything and in a very short time, thus eliminating the harvesting as our grandparents knew it.

THE FLAX HARVEST

Flax harvesting was more common in the northern counties than in any other part of Ireland, although some considerable flax crops were grown in isolated pockets in the south. When grown for fibre, it was harvested directly after the powder-blue blooms wilted, but before the flowerheads had produced seeds. The tall stalks were either harvested at the ground or pulled by the roots, and from then on were referred to as lint. Teams of farmers worked together at the flax harvesting and were known as boons. The work was particularly tough – virtually impossible for a beginner – because the tough fibrous plants were extremely hard on the hands, causing blistering and welts, and the continuous stooping was backbreaking.

A sheaf of stalks was called a beet and it contained three or four handfuls, usually bound with rushes. They were loaded onto a cart and taken to the linthole for steeping, or dubbing as it was sometimes

Below: at the flax dam

Right: scutching flax

called, so that the stalks could ret (rot) for a period of up to ten days. Peaty water was best, and when the flax was sufficiently retted a foul odour permeated the surroundings. The beets were now slimy and ugly and difficult to handle. However, once they were grassed on the green bank above the hole, they quickly dried out. Grassing was a skilled job, for individual stalks were not allowed to touch and dry into each other. Once dried, the stalks were tied into beets for a second time and carted to the bleaching-green or yard.

When the bleaching was completed, the beets were built into stook-like gaits for the final seasoning. It was soon ready for scutching – the beating which tenderised the tough stalks.

THE THRESHING

Although the harvest officially came to an end with the *meitheal* in October, many farmers worked further with the corn in wintertime. Winnowing, threshing and milling were the three winter jobs which in former times were accomplished at intervals when the weather

Right: scutching corn (Aran Islands)

was suitable. In latter times, the travelling mill combined two or more jobs during a brief visit.

The earliest method of threshing was done with the flail ('stick-and-a-half'). First of all, the corn was removed from the stack and the sheaves torn open with the toe of a boot. On primitive farms where even a flail was a luxury, the farmer scutched the corn by the handful against a boulder or stout wooden post. The threshing-frame was an improvement on this. In parts of the west where they had very small crops, the farmer scutched corn in the same way as flax farmers scutched flax, so that the grain fell to the ground but the straw remained undamaged for thatching.

When I was young, my father threshed with the flail which he had inherited from his father. He spread a sheet on the barn floor and opened out a couple of sheaves at a time for beating. As the walloping got underway, a steady rhythm developed, and he maintained it was the rhythm that kept him going later on when he was feeling tired.

In earlier times, the favourite threshing place was the kitchen floor, preferably with a front and back door open to create a draught for taking the chaff away. The chaff was the lightweight corn husks which were separated from the corn proper during the beating. A special threshing-board was kept by many farmers, who liked the hollow sound created when the flail was used on it – a horse's skull buried close to the edge of the clay floor magnified the deep sound.

Left: threshing-frame

Right top to bottom: two-man thresher;
flail hanging; scoop basket

The flail consisted of three main parts –
the handle, the mid-kipple or hanging, and
the beater (swingle or soople). The handle
was generally made from hazel and was
three-and-a-half to five feet or so in length.
In the midlands, ash wood was sometimes
used instead of hazel, but the beater was always fashioned
from holly. The mid-kipple was made from anything pliable ranging from eelskin to rawhide. My grandfather used
a thong of eelskin, which he drew between hoops of leather on
each stick. In parts of Cavan and the northern areas generally, a hole
was bored through the handle and a groove through the beater. A
similar method of tying was used in the west, using two holes instead
of one.

When the threshing was completed, the winnowing had to be
done, and in former times a winnowing tray or riddle was used. The
winnowing got rid of any remaining chaff, and the best way to do
this when using a tray or riddle was to stand
on a stool or rock and shake the container
vigorously in the wind above the head, so
that any chaff dislodged from the corn ker-
nels would drift away in the breeze. A 'sweet'
breeze was desired, even for the early winnowing-machines as they

Left top to bottom: winnowing, using a tray;
drum-winnowing machine; winnowing-machine;
threshing-mill

had sacking which flagged hard in the breeze.

The winnowing-machine combined the jobs of thresh-ing and winnowing in later models. The corn sheaves were fed into the drum, separated from the seeds inside and brought out at one end as straw. The seed came out at the other into sacks, and the chaff was blown out from a separate channel to form a featherlight mound a short distance from the machine.

Large threshing mills adopted the same principle, but were, of course, much faster and were generally powered by steam. There were many different models of threshing-machines, winnowing-machines and mills. The big mills worked on contract jobs only, but many farmers had small machines, such as hand-threshers and winnowing-machines, which they loaned to neighbours.

The day of the threshing was a big day for the farmer when the mill and its atten-dant steam engine were expected, because it meant that a whole host of helpers came along too and required feeding at the end of the day. Young children were excited at the prospect

Above: large steam-engine

for weeks, and stared awestruck when the puffing monster with its shiny brass knobs and wheels came into the yard, together with the big mill. Once the fan belt was fixed and set in motion, the mill slowly rocked into a humming rhythm that sent hens and turkeys scuttling away for cover. The work commenced, and as the sheaves were opened and turfed into the depths of the machine, the odd rat escaped and caused a minor panic amongst the men, who pursued it relentlessly with pitchforks and any available missiles. And then, as darkness fell, the men trudged into the house with keen appetites and plenty of 'ould chat'.

The grain was carted to the local watermill, or ground at home within weeks of the threshing. In former times, a quern was used to grind the corn. The quern is an ancient implement. It consists of two parts: the upper stone (which contained a hole and was sometimes referred to as a 'rocking stone' when found in a field by people who didn't know what it was and were inclined to associate it with the fairies) and the lower stone. The upper stone had a handle which was turned, bringing the stone with it over the seeds between the stones,

thus crushing them. Querns were superseded by hand-mills and corn-crushers and other small machines for home use.

The big mills were visited by the farmer when he had a decent harvest. He took a cartload of full sacks to his local miller and returned with sacks of flour and meal, the annual supply if the family wasn't a particu-larly large one. There were also a few windmills, a good example of which still stands today (not operational) in Wexford. Inside, the workings of both mills were the same – grindstones ground the corn, using the power of either water or wind. The flour when it emerged was quite warm after the milling process, and when baked in a cake was quite delicious.

Above left top to bottom: using the quern to grind corn; sackbarrow, Tacumshane windmill, County Wexford; right: watermill, County Roscommon

ACKNOWLEDGEMENTS

Most of the illustrations in this book are sketches made by the author in various museums (see below), but the author also wishes to acknowledge some works used as sources for drawings and text:

Danaher, Kevin, *Irish Vernacular Architecture*, Mercier Press (Cork, 1975).

Evans, E.E., *Irish Folk Ways*, Routledge and Kegan Paul (London, 1957).

Mercer Walker, Brian, *Shadows On Glass*, Appletree Press (Belfast, 1976).

O'Brien, Louise, *Crafts of Ireland*, Gilbert Dalton (Dublin, 1979).

O'Neill, Timothy J. M., *Life and Tradition in Rural Ireland*, Dent and Sons (London, 1977).

Shire Publications, Shire Albums, Buckinghamshire, England.

MUSEUMS IN IRELAND:

Bunratty Folk Park, County Clare.

Folk Museum, Muckross House, Killarney, County Kerry.

Irish Agricultural Museum, Johnstown Castle, County Wexford.

Knock Folk Museum, County Mayo.

Folk Museum, Glencolumbkille, County Donegal.

Pighouse Museum, County Cavan.

Ulster Folk and Transport Museum, Cultra Manor, Holywood,
County Down.

Museums in Britain

Welsh Folk Museum, St Fagans, Cardiff, Wales.

West Highland Folk Museum, Kingussie, Scotland.

Beamish Open Air Museum, near Durham, England.

Bicton Gardens Folk Museum, Devon, England.

Weald and Downland Open Air Museum, Hampshire, England.

Right: Women in shawls, Carraroe, Co. Galway

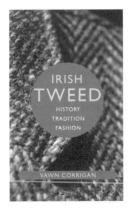

O'BRIEN IRISH HERITAGE

Dancing on the pier, Clogherhead, Co. Louth, c. 1935